GET UP AND GLOW

GET UP AND GLOW

▼

a soul full living guide

Kimberly Wyatt McDonald

Writers Club Press
San Jose New York Lincoln Shanghai

Get up and GLOW
a soul full living guide

Writers Club Press
an imprint of iUniverse.com, Inc.

For information address:
iUniverse.com, Inc.
5220 S 16th, Ste. 200
Lincoln, NE 68512
www.iuniverse.com

Cover art courtesy of Andy Doss and Jeff Spangler
Photography courtesy of Bob Lowe

The author and publisher are not engaged in rendering medical services. This book is not intended to diagnose or treat mental or physical problems. Readers are advised to seek the services of a professional or medical expert as required.

ISBN: 0-595-16040-9

Printed in the United States of America

For my husband and daughter

Contents

Preface ix

Acknowledgments xiii

Introduction xv

Section I
The Light

Chapter I

Separation 3

Chapter II

Inner World Adjustment 26

Chapter III

Love and Money 55

Chapter IV

Magnetizing 74

Section II
Expansion and Joy

Chapter V

Power Surge 89

Chapter VI

Children 111

Chapter VII
A Peace Called Home 127
Chapter VIII
Joy Above, Joy Below 141
Chapter IX
Party with God 156

PREFACE

Glow is written for every person who wishes to live exclusively in the higher realms of the human experience. If you are ready to allow that purest part of you to shine—your soul—I offer this book in service to you.

Are you ready to let go of the struggle? If the answer is yes, buckle up. You may be in for a rocky ride...temporarily. That's because the universe will nudge each one of your issues into the light for healing. This journey back to You need not be painful. It may, however, be challenging if you hold fast to ideas that are not grounded in love.

We are connected—each of us reading this book. And I can tell you that you are supported by a tremendous amount of light both above and below. If *Glow* has found its way into your hands, know that the universe is asking you to release struggle—once and for all—and move into living a life of joy.

Cuddling a baby, celebrating a wedding, reading a book, playing team sports, fixing a car...different things represent joy to different people. The common thread with every experience held in bliss: Your physical body radiates light. Whenever you move into the finer frequencies of your soul's desires, you glow. It is an effortless way to live. And it is a path that will lead you to create your own version of heaven here on earth, if you so choose.

My heart is filled with gratitude to God, Spirit, All That Is—and I use these terms interchangeably in *Glow* to represent universal love. Thank you for allowing me to be of service. To my spirit guides, thank you for keeping the faith in me. The gifts you have given me, and now to so many more people, can never be repaid. I love you so incredibly much.

This book is a compilation of everything I have learned since my mother introduced me to one of Ruth Montgomery's books at the age of ten. God bless each one of the incredible authors to whom I have been subsequently led. I am particularly indebted to the Sanaya Roman and Duane Packard titles, published by H.J. Kramer. These books, along with the Emmanuel series written by Pat Rogest and Judith Stanton, are brilliant.

A special word of thanks to author Paul Gallico. His work taught me the power of words at a young age, and changed my world.

And for my readers, remember: Everything you need to know resides within you. Use your heart to recognize your truth. Anything you read in this book that does not resonate on a deep level is not truth for you.

Listen to the voice within; hold the highest vision you can for yourself and others. Then get up and glow. I look forward to merging our collective light.

Kim McDonald
North Carolina
March, 2001

ACKNOWLEDGMENTS

A special word of thanks to iuniverse.com for the wonderful work you do. It's nice to see the publishing world democratized.

Thank you to my Canadian family for helping me remember who I am: William and Ida McDonald, Hugh John McDonald, Barbara McDonald and the always wonderful Champagnes: Denise, Marcel, Pierre and Colleen.

Thank you to my American family for doing the same: Estes and Opia Lee Wyatt, Betty Jane McDonald, Susan Lee Wyatt, and Louis and Avis Lowe. Grandmommy, thank you for bringing me home.

To the most extraordinary facilitators of spiritual growth in my life, I offer you my heartfelt gratitude: authors Ruth Montgomery, Sanaya Roman and Duane Packard. And the gifted Carol Duprez, Ph.D. and Shawna Casteel—thank you.

Bob Lowe, Brinley Lowe and kitties: You guys are awesome. I love you. I adore you.

Finally, a special word of thanks to my friends and neighbors in California for giving me a taste of the joys of community living.

Introduction

The new maxim for the 21st century is an important one: You alone are responsible for your reality. You've heard it before. What you see around you is a reflection of what you believe about yourself. Your home, your job, your relationships…you created it all. And you continue to recreate it with every new thought, deed and action.

At some level, it's an easy concept to accept. "Oh, I don't have a lot of money because I have a lot of unresolved abundance issues." Or, "I always attract loser guys because my father was a jerk." But are one person's beliefs about Self really an adequate explanation for the random cruelty that occasionally hits each of us between the eyes? Did the child of abuse draw the violence to himself through his own short life of thoughts or deeds? What about the teenager who gets gang raped on a college campus?

Perhaps you think the answer lies in karma. Some religions espouse that each of us is living a life of retribution or reward based on past deeds. If that's the case, it doesn't matter what you believe about Self: Your power, at least in this life, lies in the hands of unseen forces. Are you comfortable with that concept of destiny?

Most of us in the Western world want it both ways. We accept the idea that our thoughts create our reality…up to a point. Then tragedy occurs. We know our beliefs weren't *that* skewed. So we look for answers elsewhere: God, karma…After all, it's hard to reconcile one's individual thoughts with one's individual nightmare. Were my beliefs so wretched that I drew murder, disease or starvation to my life? The answer is no.

Painful events have transpired not because we as individuals thought "incorrectly" or came from a victimization standpoint. They've occurred because we as a unified soul group have believed one thing, and one thing very strongly: *We grow best from pain.*

Think about it. How often have you said to yourself, "That was a tough situation. But boy, did I learn a lot. I grew so much." Yikes. What are you telling the universe? You are saying very clearly that you grow a lot—through pain. Worse, your neighbor's thinking it too, and so is the next guy, and the next guy.

The human race unconsciously feeds one huge collective thought: Suffering equals spiritual growth.

When was the last time you heard someone lament, "That drug addiction was so tough. And then my wife left me. I filed for bankruptcy. But I didn't learn anything at all. I'm the same guy I was 10 years ago"? Usually the person is quick to point out the positive changes that resulted from the pain. "It made me more compassionate." "I learned that underneath we're all the same." "I'm more of a loving person now." Nothing wrong with that. Except it reinforces the belief that turmoil is still the best way to get back to You.

The universe will teach us any way we want to be taught. Whether you look at the earth as a schoolroom or a place to remember your way back to God, the soul is never idle in its attempt to direct your attention back to its essence. Who wants their growth served with a big dose of challenge and misfortune?

Most of us were not aware we had a choice. Until recently, the "growth through crisis" paradigm had been so universally entrenched we each dutifully created and took on life's slings and arrows.

We do have a choice. The times are changing. And if you in your infinite wisdom were drawn to this book, God wants to show you an easier way to live.

The great spiritualist and medium Edgar Cayce predicted that just prior to the new millennium the world would undergo revolutionary spiritual change. It has happened.

Look at your own life over the past several years. You have probably been asked—in no uncertain terms—to relinquish people, places or things not for your highest good. (And hasn't the push to do so been intense?)

Each of us is being readied to move into a life of magnificent love and joy—if we choose. We will reside in light—if we choose. And that brings us to the very real issue of choice: We can continue to grow through pain. Or we can grow without struggle, through joy. If you can open your heart and mind to the latter, this book will help you live that reality and teach others to do the same.

Section I

The Light

———————▼———————

The layers and layers of God denial that encrust most souls in physical form

cannot be removed all at once…they require the gradual wearing away of

resistance through experience. Unfortunately, many experiences are painful

and negative until a certain point, after that which the learning can progress

through light and pleasure.

—Emmanuel

CHAPTER I
SEPARATION

▼

Heaven on earth—whatever that may be for you—is attainable. But in order to achieve it you must be willing to release the need to suffer. This may be a difficult concept for you. Most of us believe that life is filled with many ups and downs, and suffering is unavoidable. Also, many of our greatest lessons have occurred in the worst of circumstances, which only serves to strengthen the "growth through pain" paradigm. The reality: strength of character, and living a life of happiness and bliss, are not mutually exclusive.

Source Separation

How do you want to live your life? Are you ready to let go of crisis-to-crisis living? If you are in constant turmoil, consider yourself separated from the Source.

What is "Source"? The source is God. You may prefer to call this energy Buddha, the Light or whatever feels like truth for you. It doesn't matter how you define it. The key is that in this vast universe we are all linked to each other, and to the Divine.

Each soul is pure love, created from God in the image of God. The tools we have picked to experience our soul—the physical body and our corresponding mental and emotional worlds—come each with its own set of needs. That's why it's easy to focus on anything but the soul when every other aspect of our self is clamoring for attention. Redirecting our focus back to our essence, and thus to the greater universal Spirit, has always been facilitated most quickly by crisis. So struggle and outright disarray tend to be the norm whenever we've moved too far away from our connection with God.

Even with the deeply ingrained belief that
pain is a part of life, most of us are stumped by the
amount of suffering we have created
—individually and as a group.

Our soul exists in another realm and yet it is always with us: lovingly and gently reminding us of who we really are. If we choose to experiment with who we are not, so be it. That is blessed, too. Our soul, as part of Spirit, honors our free will.

If, for example, we pursue only power and prestige, our higher self steps aside. If we are wooed by the surreal world of drug and alcohol abuse, our higher self steps aside. By allowing the wishes of our ego or personality to take precedence, the soul bides its time. After all, it's only a blink before we return to the only real source of inner peace: God. In the meantime, we dance the life dance.

Even with the deeply ingrained belief that pain is a part of life, most of us are stumped by the amount of suffering we have created—individually and as a group. Where is God in all this? Why would Spirit step aside when civilized countries annihilate ethnic groups and schoolchildren kill their classmates?

God has nothing to do with it. The human race has free will. We, as a collective energy, decided a long time ago that growth—return to Spirit—was facilitated best through struggle and pain. We decided we could learn more about our true essence, which is love, if we moved as far away from love as possible. Thus each of our souls has willingly chosen to add some dimension of "not God" to our life experience. By experiencing the pain of not God, we return to God. We gain clarity on exactly what we do want…when we experience what we do not want.

Almost everyone has suffered the end of a painful love affair. Think back on a particularly difficult relationship. Is that former connection compatible with the person you are now? Probably not. By experiencing pain and other things that did not reward your soul, you crystallized what would reward your soul. It may have taken several relationships of "suffering" to get it; you still may not have totally gotten it. But rest assured that you created elements of *not God* to better appreciate what in a loving relationship is *of God*.

On the other hand, knowing what is not of God does not necessarily mean reversing course. We may know what does not bring peace, yet still plug into tumultuous energies. Some individuals thrive on drama. You may know them; you may even be one of them. Choosing inner peace over disorder may not be an option for these souls at the personality level—at least not yet.

Chaos may be another group's only frame of reference. Think of individuals in war-torn or poverty-stricken countries. Many of these human beings have little understanding, again at the personality level, of anything but struggle to survive.

Other times a soul actually craves turmoil, even violence, because it offers the opportunity for jolts of growth. Gang members, terrorists and those who inflict bodily harm onto others fit into this category. Jolts of growth occur when a being exists on sheer volatility of emotion. There is such separation from the Divine that the personality needs to create utter chaos just to feel alive. This individual does grow. But it is a heavy and exhausting price to get back to the core of who they are.

Far more common are those daily battles of lesser proportions that most of us readily engage in. Not enough money to pay the bills, bickering with your spouse, the car's on its last legs, the kids are doing poorly in school…and so on. It's all just a smaller manifestation of fear and Source separation.

If you are lamenting your life and creating the same circumstances over and over again, you are operating from a place of fear. Fear of change, fear of personal growth—whatever it may be—fear is not a comfortable space. Yet you are not doing anything "wrong." The emotion of fear is no better than so-called positive emotion. It's all energy. It's how you direct that fear-based energy that will inform your life…and create for you pain or joy.

You can continue to create more of the same outer circumstances by keeping busy with distressed thoughts and feelings. Or you can create an entirely different dynamic by quieting your mind and asking for soul input. In one brief moment, your higher self will show you how to take that energy born of fear and use it to add more light to the world. The power to recreate is always in your hands.

Here's a simple example: A man feels negative emotion over his neighbor's barking dog. The dog barks all day; the man cannot concentrate on his home-based work. After weeks of brooding, the man confronts and threatens his neighbor.

Now the ripple effect begins. The neighbor's angry, too. The neighbor snaps at his wife, the man snaps at his girl-friend, the dog continues to bark. One little area of the world now pulsates murky, resentful energy. If there's an ingrained belief the two grow best through pain and strug-gle (and there probably is), who knows how long the neighbors will play out their drama?

Another course of action: The man uses the energy behind his anger to approach the neighbor in a spirit of cooperation. Maybe the neighbor does not know his dog barks all day. If the approach is to use fear-based energy to transform a situation from dark to light, then no matter what the initial emotion was, it is *joy* that carries the day.

Joy for the dog—maybe the dog ends up in doggy day school or obedience class. And joy for the two neighbors who have found a way to improve both the neighborhood energy and their relationship with each other.

Growth, or jump-start to Spirit, eventually occurs in either case. The question is, how do you want to get there: thrashing about in the dark or moving gently into the light?

The emotion of fear is no better than so-called positive emotion. It's all energy. It's how you direct that energy that will inform your life and create for you joy or pain.

If you're on the receiving end of the discontent—the neighbor—you have an option. You can remain calm and centered. Or you can react fearfully. If you think even briefly "what an idiot," your vibration lowers, you feel shaken and you've lost your balance. In effect, you've allowed yourself to be pulled into someone else's turbulence.

Have you ever been around toxic people and found yourself longing to get home and take a shower? That's one sign that your aura, or energy body, has absorbed someone else's fear. And it's cumulative. The more time spent in toxic situations, the more damage done on a vibration level. Why should that matter? Once your vibration lowers, you start attracting things of a lower nature in all aspects of your life.

"Like attracts like"; "birds of a feather flock together"; you get the idea. The same thing happens when your energy gets infused with someone else's negative output. The longer the exposure, the more effort it takes to extricate yourself from sticky, fear-based residue. Until you do, you continue to attract people, places and things of a similar discordant nature.

Let's say you have a fight with your spouse. Then your boss berates you in front of coworkers. You arrive home and your television dies. That's your day in a nutshell. Once the downward spiral starts, it picks up speed! It's like a snowball rolling downhill. You draw in even more experiences that complement your lowered vibration.

Contrast that scenario with the times, however scarce, that you've honored yourself by doing things all weekend long that bring you joy. You snuggled in bed with your children, enjoyed coffee and croissants before rising, spent time in the rose garden…Or perhaps you played with your dogs in the park, finished a good book or shared a romantic dinner with someone you love.

Whatever is joyful and nurturing for *you* clears your energy and raises your vibration. Now it's Monday morning. Notice the difference. It may be something as minor as hearing your favorite songs on the radio while driving to work. Perhaps you hit all the green lights. Suddenly your boss is agreeable. You win money in the office football pool.

That is the way energy shifts occur. Pain begets pain; joy begets joy. That's why the expression "when it rains, it pours" is unfortunately so apt. But so is the reverse. Once you commit to cocreating joy with God, your higher self will gently guide you along the path of true outer expression of your soul. That means bliss replaces struggle at every juncture, and love replaces fear. You move in the rhythm of the higher flow.

Building with Light

Even if we had known how to create heaven on earth it would have been difficult to do so, as recently as fifty years ago. Mass beliefs about growth through adversity were too firmly entrenched in our collective consciousness. We willingly embraced the most horrific of circumstances—slavery, the Holocaust, nuclear war—to remind ourselves of who we are not.

In the context of evolution, human growth through hardship makes sense. In the beginning, life was indeed "nasty, short and brutish." Mankind's sole purpose had to be disconnected from his soul purpose. One's inner world could scarcely be acknowledged, let alone explored, until we learned to meet our basic food and shelter needs. There was little time for idle contemplation of the soul.

Eventually true Masters, including Jesus, Allah and Buddha, demonstrated how to light the world in spite of coarse earth energies. As our collective awareness expanded, it became easier for the rest of us to move from the world of illusion—external life—to that which is real—inner life.

Our evolutionary blueprint has brought us to where we are today: There is a huge amount of light available to each soul seeking to express its divinity in physical form. Meditation, prayer and groups committed to worldwide healing add to the finer energies present on the earth plane.

Our bodies have undergone subtle reconstruction, too, notably in the last decade of the 20th century, so that we may shine our light more effectively.

The more time spent in toxic situations,
the more damage done on a vibration level. Once your
vibration lowers, you attract things of a lower
nature—in all aspects of your life.

Have you noticed lately that your body reacts strongly to the food you eat, expressing distinct preferences and dislikes? Do you find yourself requiring more sleep? As Sanaya Roman notes in her book *Spiritual Growth* some people report occasional heart flutters, tingling in the extremities or chest congestion. Assuming your overall health indicates nothing amiss, be still. Ask yourself if these occurrences are due to the restructuring of your physical body to hold more light.

Some of you may notice nothing different; others may be indifferent to the physical changes. Regardless of your awareness level, your chakras—or energy centers—*are* being powered-up to allow you to glow…wherever you go. This means we can infuse every instant with love. And the impact of each loving choice made has never been greater.

I can step on the snail or I can move him out of harm's way. I can let the car beside me change lanes or not. I can smile at the harried mother in the grocery store with the screaming child or I can grimace in judgment. As Mother Teresa said, "Do not think that love, in order to genuine, has to be extraordinary…Be faithful in small things because it is in them that your strength lies."

When there is a catastrophe, witness the coming together of disparate people in an effort to help their fellow earth inhabitants. At the core of every person there is righteousness. Why let your core light shine only when there is chaotic darkness surrounding you or your loved ones? Add to the brilliance of your life every day by shining light to whatever you encounter.

- Remember to be grateful for what you do have; the universe will bring you more of the same.
- Eliminate negative people from your life.
- Ask to be a healing force in the world.

If you compound your light by rejoicing when everything is going well instead of thinking, "Uh-oh, everything's going *too* well. Something bad must be about to happen" you will stay in the higher, finer energies of all that is and create the world of your dreams.

Release with Love

All pain comes from lack of connection with Spirit. If you relegate your connection with God, the Universe—or however you define Love and Light—to last place, you will be in pain. Even if you know this to be true intellectually but still choose not to live in the light, you will suffer.

Once you make a commitment to honor God within, you reflect God without. In the process, however, you may have to do some demolition. And this is where your faith may be tested.

As Louise Hay says in *You Can Heal Your Life*, the whole process is a little like cleaning a turkey pan after Thanksgiving dinner. "The pan is all burnt and crusty, so you put it in hot water and soap and let it soak for awhile. Then you begin to scrape the pan. Now you really have a mess; it looks worse than ever."

Sometimes things have to get stirred up in order to get squeaky clean. In the process of tearing down the old to live with the new, you may find yourself resisting areas of You that have not seen love in years.

Will it hurt to revisit dark memories and hold them to the light? Not if your commitment is to heal them. But this is not always easy. Those places were born and held in fear. And they vibrate at an energy level (and a memory level) that is lower and denser than anything born from love.

Be patient with yourself. You are here to live as Spirit in a physical world. And you are doing a wonderful job! God is with you every step of the way. The universe wants you to experience pleasure with every ounce of your being. If you commit to a life plan of learning through joy, you will live in bliss.

Will there be days of frustration as you turn over rocks and unearth areas of your life long since rejected? Perhaps. And will you revisit old issues you thought you could bury? Yes. But this process and residual pain will ease with time as the universe supports you in your quest to radiate love in this world. Soon your entire being will shimmer like a crystal in the sun. There will be no more rocks to turn over and no more dark places to heal in your own being—only in the world at large.

> *The universe wants you to experience pleasure with every ounce of your being. If you commit to a life plan of learning through joy, you will have bliss.*

What of grief? If one lives a life of joy, and then loses a loved one to death, how can we not say that life is painful and pain is unavoidable? A special word about grief and loss. God giveth and He taketh away. Mankind experiences the most pain when someone we love has served their time on earth and returns to a life of Spirit.

Living a life of joy does not mean you can avoid grief. God can and does call back your spouse, your child, your beloved pet…whenever the time is right for those souls to live in a different realm. If you have committed to living a life of joy, do not think you've regressed because suddenly your life is colored with sadness. Your soul did not ask for this loss in order to "grow." This is about the other being's soul, and their own spiritual map.

Your grief, however, can be mitigated by dealing with the unthinkable beforehand. What would I do if the person I love died *tonight*? Have I said everything I want to say? Have we done everything we want to do together as a couple, as a family? Does this person fully understand how much I know them to be a gift from God?

We hear a lot about how we should be living our lives as if we had only six months to live. How often do we think, "What if this person who fills my soul were to die in a few hours?" Letting this thought cross our mind every so often would result in a rejoicing of life. Bickering would be replaced by selflessness as we celebrated the best of each moment together.

When I hold my daughter, I am catapulted to unparalleled heights of joy. I adore her. She is my beautiful, wonderful baby. The reality, of course, is that she is a gift and I am a custodian of the gift. She is a child of God. When she returns to God is a matter between my daughter and the Holy Spirit. So I thank the universe for giving my husband and me this bundle of divinity, every day and in every way. And I eagerly look forward to our many years together as a family. At the same time I cherish every second with this little girl—never taking any instant for granted. I try to be fully present, one hundred percent in the moment, every time I am with this sweet, sweet soul.

When someone you love returns to Spirit, remember that in their dying there is always rebirth for both of you. For those left behind, there is now life without someone you loved. It's a new life with the same potential as your old one, only temporarily minus someone who touched your heart. Grieve the separation. Then honor the person by celebrating what they brought to your soul and to this earth.

The universe, and indeed the loved one, does not wish you to suffer. It is not a loss for the person you love. It is a gain…a gain of freedom, of new life in a rarefied state. Would you cry tears of despair if this same soul had a baby, moved into the house of their dreams or won an award? Would you lie in bed and lament how cruel the world was? No, of course not. Why suffer then when a loved one reaches one more pinnacle of joy in their existence? The reason is because you are sad for yourself.

The grief is for time lost on this earth with someone you love very much. It may be despair for things that were not said or things that were said in haste. The separation, however, is just an illusion. The spirit of the person you love is still there, closer than you realize. If you need to heal wounds with this soul, do so. Write them a letter; they will read it. Talk to them with your heart; they will hear. Bring them flowers; they will appreciate your sentiments of love.

You are growing together still, even though it may seem you are worlds apart. Your growth facilitates their growth. Likewise, their intervention on your behalf strengthens as you merge your collective energy. It is pain that holds both of you back. Reframe your grief into positive action. Say clearly, "I know you are here with me, and here's what we are going to do together on this earth. Even though I miss you, I choose love instead of pain. Let us work to…" *and then make a plan!*

This doesn't occur to most people. They think dead means gone, and whatever your loved is doing "up there" cannot comfortably coexist with whatever you're doing "down here." Not true. Set a goal; invite their cooperation.

Your plan could be as straightforward as, "I want you to help teach my children about our family history" to "I want to start an AIDS ministry in your honor." Whatever feels special for you and joyful for you, broadcast it. Then call on the assistance of the person you love for their help and participation.

Would you cry tears of despair if this same soul had a baby, moved into the house of their dreams or won an award?

The belief that once departed a soul is out of commission is simply untrue. You can still intermingle, enjoy each other's company and effect positive change in the world. Do God's work together. Your loved ones are waiting to assist you. They cannot do so if you have shrouded the light of your soul in grief.

And what of the most painful of all occurrences, when someone loses a child to death? There can be no greater heartbreak. Everyone knows this, even those who have not experienced this, the cruelest of all losses.

That soul—your child—needs to go. And you need peace. You may prefer to curl up and die, but your child needs you to live, for both of you. That is part of the deal. There are no accidents. When a child goes to the light, this is Divinity at work. God's greatest gift has been taken away, yes. That is why it is so important to cherish every moment, every second, with people you love because they could be taken in an instant. And with a child that loss defies natural order.

You can let it inform your life, so that you paint all the rest of your experiences with sorrow. But as a wise person once said: *The world would understand…your child would not.*

Do not forsake the vow you made to love and teach this child from the moment you held that baby in your arms. Show them that even with this, the most horrendous of life occurrences, a person can still live with joy. Hold up your end of the bargain. Ask your child to help you be the best parent you can be by honoring their life, not reliving their death.

When death temporarily separates you from the person you love, and you mourn and project that this person is gone forever, your emotions cast you in a cruel downward spiral. You walk yourself and your loved one a little further away from Source.

A thought is a thing. Pain fosters more pain, for both of you. Hold that pain to the light. Ask for guidance—not in letting the person go—but in letting the sadness go. Then call that person to you and draft a blueprint for the next phase of your relationship together.

If you try to get over the loss of a loved one, you are forgetting there is no loss. The soul you love is right there with you. Acknowledge that. They no longer have a physical body. How wonderful for them! And can't you feel their love? Be patient with yourself. Do what you need to do. Then when you're ready, affirm to the universe that you will go on. Not *get over*, but rather go on, having integrated this experience into your life.

We have not been taught how to let go. With few exceptions we do not readily release people, places or things. Your inner voice whispers of other possibilities, perhaps. The personality prefers not to listen. "No, I absolutely will not give up my boyfriend." Or, "A new job, no—it's better if I stay right where I am." And then the pain begins.

This desperation to resist change is particularly true when someone you love is ready to leave their physical body. Try to imagine their freedom even though you miss them. They dance with the angels and party with God. It doesn't get any better than that! In our refusal to release, we wallow. We focus on ourselves and what we perceive as a loss, rather than what it is—a transitional point in our relationship with the person we love.

Life is change. We all know this. Still we stubbornly hold on to the old and outworn because we have not been taught how to let go with ease.

Remember: That person's death was but one small facet of their life. Do not give it any more mental play than it warrants. If you find yourself ruminating over the manner of their death, let it go. It's like someone remembering your life by focusing on the day you wet your pants in kindergarten. How is that relevant to your life any more than the way you choose to make a final exit? Would you want to be defined by one small moment in time? It does not honor the life of the person you loved by staying locked in the memory of how they died.

Teach your children that death is a part of life as soon as possible. If a family pet dies, begin the instruction with a ceremonial release of your pet. Remind everyone it's okay to cry, feel sad or even numb. There is a natural grieving process after all that our minds have constructed to make it easier for our personalities to release. But do not get lost in the despair. Now is the time for Mommy and Daddy to teach the importance of letting go with love. It's a lesson your children will carry with them for the rest of their lives.

Ask your loved ones how they want to stay connected with their pet. A younger child may need only a small memento. Keeping a picture of Spot beside his bed may be soothing and all that he needs to feel comforted. An older child may understand that Spot does not have a body, but his spirit lives on. Use your judgment. If it feels right, ask: "How do you want to share your life with your pet now?" You may hear: "I jogged with Spot. I want to still feel his presence outside" to "I just want to know I can talk to my dog and he hears me."

The spirit world is alive and well, waiting for you to acknowledge its existence. Even more importantly, your loved ones—be they of the animal or human variety— would love to continue to work with you.

If you use the love that flowed between you to carry on, together still, you will have peace. Letting go does not mean the end or good-bye, it just means "we are connecting on a different level now."

The bond between you remains sacred. And the second act of the relationship begins.

Release with Peace

Release every relationship in your life with peace. Allow each connection to change form gracefully.

When your young son has to leave his best friend because your family is moving, teach him to release with peace. Remind him he can connect with his friend at any time—just by thinking of him—and that love will flow between them still.

When your daughter's boyfriend dates someone else, teach her to release with peace. This instructs growth through joy. It does not negate the temporary pain of loss. But the request for peace eases the longing. When the longing has ceased and there's an emotional equilibrium reestablished, she can reframe the relationship with gratitude in her heart.

By taking the "best of" any relationship and mentally acknowledging the gifts it bestowed, the relationship concludes with love. Any lingering pain is automatically transformed by the light. Dark memories are neither held in the aura nor at the cellular level. The partnership, however brief, has been used for the highest good of all concerned.

Life is change. We all know this. Still we stubbornly hold on to the old and outworn because we have not been taught how to let go with ease.

When I first started writing this book I found myself unable to follow my own advice. In effect, we had no place to live. Because of uncertainty in the employment area, we didn't even know if we were going to stay in California. We were moving from here to there with a baby and three cats. I finally turned to my higher self, and the gentle wisdom of those above, in desperation.

Spirit, I am having a really hard time writing because my heart is heavy. I know all this to be true but I can't even begin to tap into my seeds of joy because of the pain, self-imposed, that continues to whirl around us regarding our financial issues. I know all the right things to do, but I just want to curl up and cry. I am so sick of the confusion and uncertainty…of always being on the losing end (it seems) of life's experiences—at least vis-a-vis home, money and employment. This too shall pass, I know. But my energy is sapped. I am bored. My heart aches. I feel trapped. I am sad. I don't care. I feel like dying.

A part of you is dying and it is in the dying that life springs forth. Do you think that you are alone in your grief? When all is said and done you are a child of God and you are here to create a reality that inspires others. Are you not entitled to a few moments of grief and disappointment? Of course. Living a life of joy means finding balance, stability and integrity in your day-to-day activities. It means capturing the momentum and riding the crest of the wave. It also means that sometimes the sea will be stormy and that is when you must look within to find the joy you think is alluding you. Where is the spiritual connection: Are you alone or are you protected by the angels who love you? Right timing, right action, you know it to be true. Feel your pain but do not give into despair because it becomes a perpetuating cycle. And we have work to do. You have pictures to paint, and places to go, and people to see, like it or not. Feel your pain. Then move on and use your strength to repair and rebuild. Move into the light.

Thank you. I ask for guidance and to be an instrument that helps other people. Maybe in the process I can help myself!

Sometimes the teacher needs the lesson more...you know the saying. You are not alone. And this is what you need to realize yourself and tell your readers. When you hang your head and say, "I cannot take any more," you cry for relief. And if you allow us, we will show you a new way to deal with a situation that seems hopeless. Remember, when you transform, the angels rejoice with you because it is in that moment you become a messenger to others who also need to transform, and have lost faith in their power to do so. When you feel you are at the end of your rope, remember the universe has a Divine plan. And you are a master, a master of light, and you must accede to the plan regardless of your outer circumstances. They will take care of themselves. Do not get lost in the details when there is so much work to be done.

How can I do the work when my heart is heavy and I have a hard time believing this stuff when, is it really even working for me? I mean, geesh, it's not like I'm a good example...

Yes, you are the best kind of example, because you know the Truth, you are on the wave of change and you can invigorate people with the knowledge that they will be challenged to release their fears and self-doubts, and when they resist, the universe will stir things up like mad so they can say, "Enough. This is chaos I never want to experience again. And there is a way out. I will find my way back to the light. And in the process, I will grow with joy and achieve the life of my dreams." If something is not of the highest order, how can it be joy? It cannot be joy. It resonates with fear and the lower vibrations.

When you declare that you will live in joy, one by one your issues will be held to the light. You will be asked to transform them. Do it and do it with glee. It may seem tough going, but that's part of the process. It's like a baby learning to walk. A fall here, a tumble there. Then comes the joy, the freedom. There is walking, there is running, there is light. And look at that baby inspire all the other babies around him or her. Wow! That baby is walking. I will walk too! And so it is. The other non-walking babies will feel frustration, they may pout, they may get discouraged, but ultimately they will accomplish what they need to do. It's in their blueprint. It's part of the master plan. How easy it is for them depends on them. Fortunately, it's always easier when others are around to say, "I did it. And you can too." Do not ever underestimate the power of transformation through inspiration.

Okay, thank you. I just want to make sure this book is relevant. I want to know that this book has meaningful information that can reform outdated beliefs. And if I'm saying, "Hey you can grow through joy, without struggle" and yet I'm experiencing all the things I'm telling my readers they don't have to experience, how on earth is what I'm doing worth anything. It's like, "Oh hey, it can be done, but guess what, I can't do it, so good luck, hope you can."

You have done it and you continue to do it every time you get on the computer. Look at your level of joy compared to where it was five years ago. The potential is there for you to create heaven on earth and it grows stronger every day. The misconception is that you can have joy in every area of your life without a clearing. If you look at areas of your life where you most want and desire joy, that's usually a clue as to where there is the most stagnant, low energy vibe. You will feel the low energy vibe even more strongly because it stands in such contrast to the areas of your life that are joyful. If everything is negative, or of a low energy vibration, it's all a muted hum. If some areas of your life hit glorious notes, it contrasts dramatically with those areas that have little music. Do you see what we mean? The people who are drawn to read your book are those who have done much introspection already.

When they want to bring in more joy, the likelihood is they have most of their life working already. These are not neophytes. These are sophisticated seekers like yourself who are ready to move to the next stage of development and literally save the world from the hazy pollution of negativity that continues to obscure light and love. Fear not! You will not be misleading or obscuring the reality of transformation. Anything that is not of the highest order is not joy. Period. If you want joy in every area of your life, clearing must occur in places that have been left dormant, festering and unchanged.

Thank you, Spirit. I guess it would be futile for me to ask if you see anything of a bright horizon for us—since so much of it is self-determined.

Very true, and so much of it is also gently guided by those who know better than you at this moment what is best for you and for your family. Our advice is to focus on the love. The love that flows through your home can be expressed anywhere, and no one will feel needy. That is your fear. And we hear the concern and the heartache over the movement and the upset you think may result to various members of the family. The reality is that if you are calm and centered, all will be well.

You see, when you speak with love and when you act from love, there is love. You can't help but be in the higher flow. When you work and ask to influence with love, you can't help but influence with love. Focus on taking the hands of the guides and angels who are here to help you and your loved ones. Continue the meditation. And do not project fear or be too hard on yourself when there is so much at stake right now. The winds of change whirl around you, and you need only know that all is well in your heart and soul to withstand any minor tousling from the surrounding air.

CHAPTER II
INNER WORLD ADJUSTMENT

───────────▼───────────

Once you commit to living a life of joy, know that anything that is not for your highest good will fall away. Anything—job, home or relationship—will change form if it is not operating at its most elevated state.

How do you know if something is or is not of the highest order? You need only assess the situation briefly. Does it feel like struggle or does it feel light? Do I have more or less inner peace with this person or job? Does my home radiate love—or darker energies, such as anger and resentment?

Inspect and conclude on your own. Otherwise, you may be surprised when Spirit gently, and then a little more forcefully, shows you a better way.

It does not have to be difficult to weed out what is not working in your life. And Spirit is always waiting for us with love and compassion whenever we cannot take the havoc we've created. All it takes is one different decision: "Help me, please." And your soul, using the light of God, will start to broadcast healing images to move you up and out of your desperate situation.

Thus a relationship with a parent, child, lover or friend that does not reside in light cannot coexist with the rest of your life that is light. The universe will ask you to change the form by taking the relationship to a higher level—or by releasing it with love. Likewise, if you are pursuing a career path that feels heavy, the universe will prod you to radically transform the situation or get a new job.

If you are struggling with anyone or anything, the universe will make it increasingly uncomfortable for you.

> *The universe will never take away from you without giving you something better.*

Once you do make a shift in consciousness, your personal power will unfold before you in ways you never thought possible. As soon as you create from love—pursuing your highest good—it becomes the highest good for everyone involved.

Remember: *The universe will never take away from you without giving you something better.* Think of the times you were frightened of change—leaving a relationship, for example, or making a move. Notice how the universe came through for you. Maybe you faced turbulence initially but eventually that change gave you a great gift. Perhaps it allowed you to experience more inner peace, live with more freedom or make a contribution to others in a similar set of circumstances.

God, Buddha, Spirit...whatever you perceive as Light and Love in this world is perfect. And you will always be guided with as much love as you are open to receive.

If you cannot release behavioral patterns or you find
that certain events always push your buttons—regardless
of how committed you are to change—you're stuck.

Present circumstances are always conditioned by childhood experiences. That is a given. But somewhere between
the ages of eighteen and twenty-one the dynamic shifts.
And the power to create our own life, instead of primarily
react to the one created by our parents, becomes something we need to own.

If you can get clear on your own—reading books or
talking with friends—that's wonderful. The problem is
more deep-rooted when you continue to replay an
unhappy situation over and over. The players may be different. But the situation or emotions are the same. If this is
true for you, consider therapy as means of preliminary
self-transformation.

People avoid therapy for a variety of reasons but most
of it boils down to fear: fear of being blamed, fear of reliving the past, fear of being judged and fear of change.
Know there is not much you can tell your therapist they
have not heard before. You will have to do the work, however. And that bothers many people. It's difficult to switch
from a victim mindset—where everyone has done it "to
you"—to a person of power.

In Robert Monroe's book *Far Journeys*, Monroe's
otherworldly experiences indicate that psychologists,
psychiatrists and social workers rank number one as
facilitators of spiritual growth in our world. That's because
the majority of counselors have committed at a soul level
to transform lives through love. This is not going to be
true in every case, of course. That is why it's critical to do
your research and ask for assistance from a higher power

before seeking help. Once you do find the right professional, you can expect to be supported in a nurturing environment and for deep healing to occur.

If this resonates as truth for you, mentally affirm that you will connect with the highest possible therapeutic professional. Then turn it over to your spirit guides before you go to sleep tonight.

Be prepared for miracles here. As long as you commit to face the pain head-on in order to release it, you've taken the first step to living a life of peace—and achieving personal growth through joy.

By Design

There are no random occurrences. Everything that happens to us is by our own design. Your parents, childhood circumstances and genetic makeup were picked long before you were born. And you planned with maximum attention to detail. Much like an artist carefully selects the proper canvas, paintbrushes and colors, you picked the tools that were perfect for your life's incarnation.

Most of us at one time or another have begged God to know why we picked this particular family or that particular body. Love it all.

In the case of families, there is often a soul link with family members—perhaps one in particular. Other times there is no such link, but rather a desire to feel like a fish out of water with a different soul group. Sometimes the genetic code of a particular mother/father coupling is too good to pass up. You may need it for your life's work. In any case, bless it, honor it and thank God for the opportunities these tools have afforded you.

The reality is that your outer circumstances, including your body, were constructed as instruments of the Divine. Your choices were not made with ambiguity. You chose to come to the earthly plane to facilitate growth not just for yourself but for others as well. You picked a vehicle that allows you to express the full extent of who you are now, and who you plan to be in the future. The planning was extensive.

Beyond the obvious choice of race and socioeconomic status, many of you ponder why you picked a big nose, for example, or a short stature. Remember that the earth plane is a superficial one. The outward appearance you affect is designed more to elicit other people's reaction to you rather than for your own particular convenience or inconvenience.

You designed your body with the guiding hand of Spirit. Enjoy it, enhance it and fill it with even more light by focusing on the gifts you came to share with others.

An exceptionally beautiful physical body may be picked by a soul who is grounded very much in the physical realm. What a challenge then to turn one's attention inward when everyone else is preoccupied with the external. If this soul can remember its way back to compassion and love—when the rest of the world is enamored with his or her physical body—you are looking at a great deal of spiritual progress indeed.

A less-than-pleasing physique is often chosen to enable a soul to get down to business with minimal distraction. In some ways, the so-called less attractive person—with little attention focused on their outward appearance—is able to work more efficiently doing things that are important and life-affirming. The outside world is not paying as much attention to the outer shell, thus the soul likewise tends to get on with core matters.

If a person chooses a startling appearance, through deformity or disease, the soul is most likely an "accelerator." An accelerator comes to the planet to demonstrate that any obstacle can be overcome, and that the light of the soul does not need a so-called perfect body from which to shine forth. Like everyone else, it may take this soul's personality a while to remember its way back to its glorious essence. But once it does, the person with the dramatically different appearance has the ability to radically change lives.

This should not be taken to mean that if you really want to live as Spirit in the material world you need to look rather ordinary or even displeasing. On the contrary. Your body is a magnificent work of art. Whether or not your particular look conforms to societal standards of attractive is neither here nor there. You are light and you are beautiful. And because your body and outward countenance change with every thought you have, you have the potential to blow away a room with your essence—anytime, any place.

You designed your body with the guiding hand of Spirit. Enjoy it, enhance it and fill it with even more light by focusing on the gifts you came to this earth to share with others. It's all right to pamper and preen. Nature does it all the time—flashing brilliant arrays of color and bold displays of vanity. Exalt in the glory that is you. And remember to affirm that your body is an extension of the light within.

Picking bodies, parents and places to live before birth invariably raises the issue of destiny versus free will. If I have picked absolutely everything, even down to the size of my big toe, does that mean I've already picked my spouse and my children, too—before I came to this planet?

Here's the paradox…yes, but there is free will. You came with a general plan, but if you choose to create a new one that's your prerogative. You can run for president of the United States or you can rob the local convenience store. Neither your higher self nor God will stop you from pursuing whatever you wish.

If, however, something is not for your higher good, you will gently be shown a better way. The choice is then up to you. You can listen to the voice within or push against the current. Since most people do not like mayhem and chaos, eventually they find themselves once again in accordance with their highest possible life plan. But the time frame is usually quite flexible.

Some personalities need very little prodding to align themselves with the greater good. Others are more rigid in their attachments and find it difficult to move into the higher flow. As Kahlil Gibran wrote, "In your longing for your giant self lies your goodness: and that longing is in all of you. But in some of you that longing is a torrent rushing with might to the sea, carrying the secrets of the hillsides and the songs of the forests. And in others it is a flat stream that loses itself in angles and bends and lingers before it reaches the shore."

*You came with a general plan, but if you
choose to create a new one that's your prerogative.
You can run for president of the United States or you can
rob the local convenience store.*

Looking back over the course of your life it's usually easy to see what was strongly encouraged by your higher self and what was not. Anything in your life that involves the significant needs of others is not random.

If children are waiting to be born to you (and your future spouse) for genetic reasons or due to a strong familial soul link, you will find yourself beckoned by the universe to take steps to connect with the right man or woman. Chance meetings and coincidences are really nonexistent at this level. You are dealing with an important part of the tapestry that is more than just a symbolic coming together of two lives.

On the other hand, what you do with that relationship is entirely up to you. It is not predestined that you and a mate will spend 50 years together or even one. On the contrary, you are creating mutually diverse spiritual needs every moment that you speak and act. Your relationship is being redefined on a daily basis depending on your actions and the actions of your loved one.

So when you hear the expression "grow apart," it is not just a matter of superficial interests drawing you in different directions. It's also about soul motivations that no longer intersect.

Some of us spend time lamenting what was or was not in prior relationships. "What a waste of time" or "If only I'd…" Bless these relationships. They gave you the tools to create more joyful couplings down the line. If you were wronged in the past, accept responsibility. That's how you chose to grow then: through pain. It does not have to be that way in the future, but that is what served you in the past. Start now to release any anger or expectations that future relationships will travel the same course.

Be careful, though. When self-esteem issues remain unresolved, you will attract people with similar problems. And that is not going to be joyful. Work it out—through therapy, prayer—whatever feels right for you. The clearer you get, the easier it is to keep your emotional body calm and centered. And that balance is what allows you to stay in the higher flow—attracting wonderful experiences in all aspects of your life.

Honor yourself at all times, on every issue. Too often we do things at the behest of others when there is nothing positive about allocating our time in that manner. If something feels like a struggle or a "should do," the universe is sending you a very clear message: don't do.

You may be asked to attend a social function that holds no interest for you. If it feels heavy, it's not for your higher good. Politely decline. How often have you found yourself thinking you've got to go grocery shopping, even when it feels like a struggle just to get off the couch? A seemingly minor matter, but what message do you think the universe is sending? Now is not the right time to go. Wait until it feels light to go or even joyful to go. By honoring all your feelings—even those related to seemingly insignificant matters—you always act in accordance with your highest good.

If, for example, you're hiring an employee because she looks good on paper, ask yourself if you're making the choice because you should, or if it feels light and easy to go with this person. Most of us do this intuitively whether we realize it or not.

Several years ago we had the opportunity to work with a technical editor who was making a wonderful contribution to our computer magazine. His wealth of high tech knowledge was unprecedented. When the universe had different plans for both parties, we did what felt light and joyful under the circumstances: we released. We could have made special arrangements for deadlines and the like, but it felt like a should do rather than a want to. At the time we attributed a good part of the magazine's success to this man's work. It would have been easy to allow a healthy dose of fear to take over. Fortunately, we were too busy to worry and wallow.

The very next day we worked a local computer trade show. Next to our booth was the booth of a pleasant young man who not only was a computer genius, but a writer to boot. After reviewing his material, we hired our next technical editor. This talented man performed outstanding work for our company for many years.

Honor your trepidation. Reluctance, ambivalence and struggle are messages from your soul that the universe has a better option for you.

Do not confuse a heavy feeling with plain old fear, though. There's a big difference between waiting for a better time to finish a term paper versus generalized anxiety about writing a good paper. Make sure you are very clear on this. Otherwise the paper does not get written because what you thought was bad timing (or struggle) was really fear.

Another way people dishonor themselves is by hoping to interact at a higher level with people who are not interested in a lighter exchange. If you are trying to elevate a relationship and meeting resistance, stop. It is not for your higher good. Remember the saying: *People changed against their will are of the same opinion still.* Send love and release the need to uplift. Eventually you will find yourself less drained and able to channel your efforts into causes where you *can* add more love and splendor. (And get it back, too).

Love, love, love. At a distance if you must.
It is not your obligation to interact with a person who chooses fear and anger.

This is another way of saying that sometimes we need to erect boundaries against lower vibrations. Love, love, love. At a distance if you must. It's not your obligation to interact with someone who chooses fear and anger as a means of navigating life. This serves no-one, and in fact drops the vibration of both parties.

It's not that any one person on this earth is better than another. We are all God. We were all created from God and in God's image. And each of our souls is perfect. It's also true that with the concept of free will comes the ability to make choices of a lower nature. Is the murderer inherently worse than you or me? No, but his personality choices stem from fear and anger, and therefore his energy vibrates accordingly.

Until you are able to take someone else's heavy energy, transform it and release it as light, you are under no obligation to deal with people who allow unresolved issues to run their lives.

Chances are you're not attracting a lot of souls in turmoil but if you do, something within you is asking to be healed. Sometimes that healing, or demonstration of self-love, means setting a boundary.

There is no moral imperative to help people who do not want to get out of the abyss—whether they be family members, friends, acquaintances or coworkers. Even the glorious Mother Teresa did not spend time helping people unwilling to receive. She worked with souls who opened to her with gratitude, not derision or disdain.

You may not have all the love in your heart that Mother Teresa gave so freely to others—yet—but you are a being of love and light. You do have much goodness to offer the world: much, much more than you realize. Spread your joy to all, but direct your love only to where it is warmly received.

If you honor yourself in all ways and give only to those people who honor you in return, you have made the most important inner world adjustment of all. Then, when and if negative circumstances do arise, you will be quick to ask, "Is this person criticizing me because I am critical of myself? Does this person act disrespectful to me because I did not honor myself on some level?" And you will move beyond your initial stressful energy with a newfound sense of peace and understanding.

Recently I allowed someone I love to rage at me. I understood his pain so I accepted the anger. A few hours later, a woman butted in line behind me at the grocery store. She stood so close to me that her arm was literally pushing my arm as I wrote the check. Rude? Disrespectful? Violation of my personal boundaries? You bet. Not that different from the encounter with my loved one.

People are mirrors for us. If you find yourself on the constant end of less-than-loving interactions with others, you are being less than loving with yourself. The universe is preparing you to move beyond it, to be sure. But first you need to assess the situation to intuit what the universe is trying to tell you. Then commit to change your own inner dialogue and behavior.

Chances are you're not attracting a lot of souls in turmoil but if you do, something within you is asking to be healed.

I got the message right away with the grocery store incident and set an immediate boundary. "We will seek a higher solution to this problem; we will infuse the situation with light. You will not, however, rage at me with fear and anger on this issue again." There was a shift in my consciousness, which created a shift in the other person's. Our relationship immediately moved into a higher flow.

Was the issue resolved? No, it was not. It resurfaced again, testing my commitment to my beliefs and core values. This will happen over and over until the universe is satisfied you have moved the situation into as much light and love as possible. At that point, either the relationship between players shifts entirely. Or you will be encouraged to move on if the relationship is no longer for your higher good.

On a superficial level it's easy to finger point when you find yourself being treated in a way that seems unfair or even meanspirited. But if you look at the situation carefully, you created it. You drew the situation to you as a wake up call. The universe is asking you to take stock: Is this the way you want to live? Do you choose joy or fear? Inner peace or mayhem?

One man spent so much time doing for his boss and workplace he had nothing left to give himself. His love life faltered, he was passed over for promotion, and eventually the slide of ill will and resentment began. The perpetrator of this scenario: the man himself. By looking for outside validation of his worthiness (from a job), he gave away his power. The universe sent him all sorts of situations that reaffirmed his beliefs of: "I don't think I'm good enough. Do you?"

Once you love yourself and your cup is overflowing, there is a proper acknowledgment of self transmitted to the world. "I am worthy. I do matter. My time is important. I am of God."

The universe reflects your new attitude back to you. The people who treated you with disrespect will no longer be attracted by your energy. Instead they will be drawn to others who shared your former beliefs.

Physical Healing

Illness is distorted thinking manifest. You are perfect. You always have been. If you are dealing with an untenable physical situation, correct the underlying beliefs that have now manifested in physical form. Reach back to ascertain where your thoughts were not in alignment with love.

When did you start believing you were less-than? When did you forget you were Divine? What did that emotional pain feel like? Write it down. Let it go. Release it into the light. And remind yourself that your body does not need to hold these thoughts anymore to get your attention. You see the distortion. And the illusion that you are anything but of God has been put to rest.

The deep-seated conviction that we grow best from pain is an old model. It no longer applies to you. Replace it with the assertion that from this point on you grow only through joy.

To begin the healing process, praise every creation in your life right now that reflects self-love. Anything that brings you pleasure needs to be acknowledged and appreciated. The immediate response of the universe is to give you more of the same. And by focusing on the positive in your life, your energy field is immediately lightened. This means the physical or emotional distortions can be observed from a more detached perspective—with a more enlightened solution forthcoming.

Watch your thoughts—at all times. Telling the universe what you're grateful for, then swinging back to thoughts of despair, undoes some of the good work. That's why it's important to give yourself many stress-free interludes a day to connect with God. Keep the channel open to what's real and what's true.

All healing—emotional and physical—comes from within. Scientists tell us that every two years cell regeneration literally gives us a new body. If that's the case, why do we continue to manifest the same aches and pains? Because our cells are programmed by unresolved emotional baggage. Thoughts and experiences, especially repressed anger, wreak havoc on our bodies.

This does not negate the genetic predisposition many of us carry for illness. Each family has its own collective thought system that passes through the generations with corresponding physical manifestations. The two—individual thought patterns and a group energy of illness—effectively "program" our cells.

Look at the health issues your parents faced, emotional and physical. Now look at your grandparents. Can you discern any patterns? Look beyond the obvious of chronic illness or substance abuse. You may see less obvious trends including erratic behavior, eating disorders or other issues that run like roots through your family tree.

To reverse course, consciously opt out of the family pattern. On some level the dis-ease may serve you. Or you may have thought it would serve you in this lifetime. Since God gives us free will, however, make a different decision. Pinpoint what you would have gained from the illness by looking at other family members. Decide how they grew from the experience. Write it down. Then release.

Be sure to thank your relatives for their sacrifice and inspiration. Acknowledge that while they chose to grow through pain—and you respect that choice—you are choosing a different path. You are returning to the essence that is you through joy. You do not need to partake in any prearranged family pattern to get back to your divinity.

As for illnesses that seem to have no genetic link, say chronic back pain or a persistently stiff neck...what's bugging you? If you carry a problem long enough, it eventually moves from your emotional field to your energy field. Your energy field is the human aura that surrounds your physical body. As soon as distorted thought patterns settle in your energy, it is just a matter of time before these beliefs manifest physically.

Emotional damage can be easy to ignore;
physical pain is not. The universe is perfect. It wants
you to be healed and whole.

Emotional damage can be easy to ignore, physical pain
is not. The universe is perfect. It wants you to be healed
and whole. And if you can't or won't do the work, the universe knows that physical pain will direct your attention
back to the spiritual malaise that needs to be addressed.

Dr. John Sarno's best selling book *Healing Back Pain*
tackles this subject head-on. Release the unresolved issues,
release the back pain. End of discussion. No surgery, no
physical therapy needed—no matter how debilitating
your back and neck problems appear to be. Sarno claims a
ninety percent success rate. You don't have to be a believer
in the mind/body connection to get started. My husband
picked up the book with a certain degree of skepticism.
His chronic back pain improved immediately and then
disappeared in a matter of days.

Several years later, ABC's news program *20/20* profiled
Dr. Sarno. It scheduled a repeat of the broadcast for later
that summer. I could hardly wait. There were several people I knew who were suffering terrible back pain. An
impartial investigative piece might help each of them help
themselves. One gentle man in particular was seeing a chi-
ropractor without success, trudging to the Jacuzzi every
night. I really wanted this guy to feel better. His response
to the show? Something along the lines of, "What a
quack." Whoa. It was a good reminder. Everyone is exactly
where they need and want to be.

Time and time again, Spirit will nudge us to resolve
underlying issues so that we may live a more soul *full* and

physically satisfying life. We can listen to the voice within or not. But one thing is clear: Seething emotion can only be repressed for so long before that energy finds a place in your body to demand your attention. A woman refuses to examine the oral sexual abuse she suffered at the hands of male relative. Yet she implores her physician to cure her of her inability to keep food down because her throat constricts and lately she's been gagging.

Every unresolved issue seeks to be healed in the light. The universe will repeatedly try and get your attention, sometimes with obvious symbolism. Be gentle with yourself. Stay open to the message. Ask what your body is trying to resolve. It may be an old issue only now surfacing to be healed, or it may be an ongoing problem that is getting more desperate to get your attention.

If you are so grounded in fear that you shut out the information, you will begin to see more physical manifestations of the lack of light. Everything will start to feel heavy.

When you hear people say, "I had to drag myself out of bed every morning to go into work," they are not kidding. The struggle to feel light in a situation that has outlived one's use is palpable. The body becomes sluggish; you may feel like you're caught in a vise. This is your body's way of saying it cannot abide the emotional ill will it's being asked to contain vis-a-vis a job, relationship or any other situation that is not for your higher good.

Of course, it's not always possible to transform a situation at the drop of a hat. You need only make a mental commitment to live in the higher flow. That decision, and your pledge to listen for cues and take the appropriate steps as opportunities arise, is enough for the universe to reverse course.

Now is the time to turn inward and ask for guidance. This is also the time many of us will have our faith tested. You may feel God isn't listening to your prayers. Are you listening to God? The messages are always there. If you have the courage to listen, the information will lead you to more joy and fulfillment. The problem is many of us do not listen. And we stubbornly hold on to things that no longer serve us.

If you feel abandoned by God and in an untenable situation, acknowledge your feelings. Feel the fear. Feel the anger or the frustration. It's okay to feel ripped off, fed up, unappreciated and mad. It's okay to think you'll lose it if just more thing is thrown your way.

Then commit to inner peace. Surrender to Spirit. "Gee God, whatever I've been doing thus far has not worked. Let's work *together* to find a better way."

Some people do not want inner peace. They think they do, but suffering pays big dividends. The constant turmoil frees them from having to do the work they need to do to release the suffering. The fear of examining the choices they've made—and then making the appropriate changes—is scarier than being stuck.

Feel the anger or the frustration. It's okay to feel ripped off, fed up, unappreciated and mad. It's okay to think you'll lose it if just one more thing is thrown your way.

It's okay if you're stuck. There is a way out. But heed the wisdom in the following expression: "The definition of insanity is doing the same thing over and over, and expecting different results."

Sometimes people wear their physical pain like a badge of honor—detailing aches and pains—almost in a contest of one-upmanship with fellow sufferers. Be careful. At first it may feel good to have other people commiserate. Misery loves company. The problem is you get what you focus on. The dialogue becomes a bad habit. Then, when presented with possible solutions, the personality isn't ready to release the identity of "one with back pain" or "one with digestive problems." Complaining to fellow sufferers has only served to reinforce that identity, entrenching it more firmly in your mind.

Then there's the other extreme of people who just want to rid themselves of the disorder without listening to the message it came to impart. Who can blame them? We are here on earth creating life art. Why would anyone paint with pain and despair? "I do not want this cancer. I did not choose this cancer. Get out!" Who among us hasn't thought something similar when dealing with an exhausting physical situation?

Despite your frustration, treat yourself with love—at all times—but especially when you're sick. Allow that love to bathe each one of your cells. Trust the universe. Ask for angels to assist you in your healing.

Based on your past beliefs, the universe and your soul have deemed this is your downtime. Use it to pray, refocus your priorities and choose a better way to live.

If you have to be flat on your back, so be it. Flat on your back and spiritually soaring can comfortably coexist. The key is to give your body whatever it needs to ultimately hold and radiate more light. Medication, physical therapy, bed rest—whatever the prescription—respectfully oblige. God never haphazardly holds you back. It is for your highest good that the focus is temporarily shifting to your body.

As your physical self heals, keep your mind quiet. Still the chatter. You don't want it to interfere with your body's need to rebalance. Make sure your home or wherever you are recuperating is harmonious. Incorporate natural light, plants and water—perhaps a fish tank or indoor fountain. Adorn your dresser with photos of friends and loved ones. Invite your pets, spouse and children to be with you here whenever possible.

Keep a window partially open during the day to bring in fresh air. Light candles, but only when you're well enough to know you won't fall asleep while they burn. Medications should stay in the bathroom. Looking at them on your night stand is counterproductive. It reinforces the notion of "sick" versus healed. Instead, have someone bring you fresh flowers to put on your bedside table.

If you are motivated to read, surround yourself with the most uplifting spiritual material you can find. Keep books—or whatever gives you a lift—by your side. Your body probably feels the polar opposite, so keep your healing environment vibrant.

Remember: This too shall pass. You will have a shift of consciousness. Make the most of the downtime. Don't just grin and bear it. Listen to the message. What are you gaining from this experience? How does this discomfort get you back to the core of who you are? Remind yourself of what you came to this planet to accomplish. Reaffirm that you now attract light and grow only through joy.

Do not attach yourself to any specific outcome except a positive transformation. Affirm that you will experience the highest level of healing and that you will survive with inner peace.

God knows how to use you to light the world. You may be asked to serve as a beacon in a sea of others experiencing your same illness. You may be asked to inspire by demonstrating a full recovery through dietary changes, acupuncture, prayer or yoga...the list is endless. Trust the universe to use you as you can best be used.

Do not be rigid in how you must be healed. One beautiful women with a two-year-old child was losing her eyesight to a retinal disease. She said she prayed and hoped that God would heal her. This mother, however, would not consider alternative means of healing fearing it would not be coming directly from God.

Be open! The universe uses doctors, healers, animals, the Internet, all sorts of different mediums to heal with love. Darkness (or however you choose to personify that which is not God) and healing are mutually exclusive. All healing comes from the Light. If you want the Light in your life, do not put restrictions on how it must arrive.

Use the downtime to remind yourself of what you came to this planet to accomplish. Reaffirm that you now attract light and grow only through joy.

And remember this: *You are loved, you are cared for and you are not alone.* Do not struggle. Take comfort in the arms of the God. Feel the embrace and the love that surrounds you even when the moment seems bleakest.

As I struggled, wailed and thrashed about during a troubled physical time, my inner voice said very clearly, "It's always darkest before the dawn." My response was, "Fine, what time is it now?" And I would hear, "2:00 a.m." A few months later, I would hear "3:00 a.m." It was kind of a playful way, during a trying time, to reassure me that eventually it would be 6:00 a.m. and the self-created dark night would end, once and for all.

Gratitude for the small things when the big things seem out of control is a start to building a better future. Spending a lot of time in the darkness cursing the darkness is not how dense areas get illuminated. Darkness yields to light when you remember who you are. You are a part of God. Maybe your choices have not always been Spirit-inspired, but that does not make you any less of God.

Call on the universe to direct you to the most gifted doctors and healers. And do not forget to thank the universe every time you stumble across a piece of information that may prove useful in your recovery. When I was going through my self-created misery, I suddenly jumped up out of the blue and drove to the bookstore. The first book I opened gave me information never even mentioned by my doctor. That information led to the next phase of healing and ultimately to the end of my discomfort.

When you've had enough of the dark night terrors, stand before the fear. Don't push it away. Wrap your arms around this energy. Acknowledge its pain. Soothe the darkness as you would a frightened animal. Then take it to the light. (See the exercise at the end of this chapter.)

Visualize yourself peaceful, prosperous and joyful. Allow your subconscious and God's guiding hand to manifest that reality for you.

In the final stages of healing, take the elements of your healing room and build a small sanctuary for yourself in your home or garden. Fill it with the things you love and that represent love for you: flowers, candles, pictures of your loved ones. Take a daily trip there to replenish your soul. It's important preventive medicine.

When everything is near to being back in its proper perspective and you feel better, ask to be a receptacle of love. Commit to serve others. Let the experience you've come through be a springboard to do so. The circle is then complete.

Power to Change

Growth through suffering is not inevitable. Remind yourself of that. Since most of us have been taught that the greatest lessons come from the greatest pain, it takes awhile for a new spiritual model to shift into place.

If something unexpected happens, remember that the universe is providing you with a platform to experience your total power—by allowing you to feel the polar opposite. *You do not need to feel powerless to remember the power that is you.* Declare that here and now. It works, yes. But we do not need the darkness to get from point A to B.

I can walk to the grocery store, 10 miles from my home, and carry groceries home to feed my family. Or I can drive. It's my choice. The end result is the same: Food arrives on the table.

In the end, we can appreciate the bounty of the food and the abundance of the universe with tired arms and blistered feet—or without.

Do I need to suffer and sweat to get that food home? Not unless I want to. And I don't want to. What would I have learned from that experience that I would not have learned driving there? That depends on where I am spiritually. Maybe I need that walk day after day—with armloads full of groceries—to remind me of exactly how tough and resilient I am.

Maybe I need the walk to get clarity on what I do want (comfort) by experiencing what I do not want (discomfort). Here's the key: In the end, we can appreciate the bounty of the food and the abundance of the universe with tired arms and blistered feet—or without. The choice is yours. It always is. And you're the only one making the final decision.

You can ask to be an instrument for the highest possible good of all concerned in every situation, or you can muddle through. The way you live your life can stand as an immediate tribute to God, or you can dabble deeper in darkness until you feel comfortable exercising your personal power. Either way the universe is always on standby, ready to show you a more glorious, easier, fun way to live.

Any help you wish for will be forthcoming—lovingly and with compassion—when you are ready to receive it. You will fall only as far as you choose to fall. And sometimes you'll get up and fall again, and that's okay, too. Simply listen to the tiny voice within to regain your balance. Ask for direction and support as soon as you get weary of the repeated scraped knees.

So many times we do not ask for relief. We just gripe and suffer as though that were a part of our destiny. Turn your suffering over to Spirit. Proceed with the confidence that not only will your prayers be answered, but you will experience a delightful shift in consciousness. Then turn inward and upward with open arms.

When the pain is too much to bear, and relief is not coming fast enough, some among us consider suicide. It's an issue laden with intense emotion. Whose body is it after all? How can we say God gives us free will, but don't choose suicide because if you do you've just sentenced your soul to hell? Does the state have a right to tell me if and when I can end my life?

There is no absolute here. The terminally ill senior is a different story from the teenager distraught over a relationship breakup. And both of these experiences differ from the accidental drug overdose of an addict. The one thing they do have in common: opportunity lost.

There is a way out of the darkness. And you always have the ability to bring more light into this world as long as you're alive. Even if you're just lying in bed all day "getting through it," you are ahead of the game. You're still here. And the angels applaud you for your courage.

Because souls have chosen to create so much pain and darkness to remember who they are, there is that one second in time when it is easy to forget the sanctity of life. Remember: *Every earthly problem has a solution.* If a soul destroys his or her body, it is in violation of a sacred pact that we made with ourselves and God.

There is a time to be born and there is a time to die. During our time on earth we came to create. If we create with pain and severity, the universe will support us. If we create with light and expansion, the universe will support us here, too—encouraging us to change colors only when our soul could be better served with a different palette.

There is a way out of the darkness. And you always have the ability to bring more light into this world as long as you're alive.

We are born with the basics: a time frame, a genetic code for the ideal physical body, specific parents, socioeconomic status and country of origin. All are sacred ingredients. If we disrupt the time frame by committing suicide, it's like ripping a partially completed painting down the middle. Who knows what inspirational artwork might have followed? To which the terminally ill senior citizen may reply, "Hey, I finished my masterpiece a long time ago." It may seem that way. The truth is there's always more light that can be added to the world as long as you're alive.

Exactly how much does a gravely ill person remind family and friends about what's important in life? Dying with dignity is one thing; there is also teaching others to live with dignity in situations that have very little dignity about them. The deep levels of compassion that family members must sustain when dealing with a terminally ill loved one are perhaps unprecedented. These profound life experiences—springboards back to what is important—are taken away when someone declares the jig is up, before it really is.

On the other hand, a person does not need to agonize through endless physical pain to teach the lesson. The dying in and of itself is enough to provide the instruction. Higher doses of manmade drugs could alleviate the physical torment so many terminally ill patients face during their last months on earth. This is a controversial issue. Yet many physicians readily acknowledge that needless suffering goes on. Loving and profound spiritual exchanges can and do take place without a terminally ill person needing to be in unbearable pain.

Meanwhile, the suicide of a young person is especially heartbreaking. Any person over the age of 18 knows that life is filled with surprises and good things we could not even imagine when we were young. Drug and alcohol abuse, depression...again, every problem has an earthly solution. Once the body is abandoned through suicide, the issues remain, without an appropriate forum for resolution. It is a very difficult set of circumstances. The suicide victim is not "punished" when the body is relinquished, but neither does this soul get the relief he is seeking out of body.

For those who have lost a loved one to suicide, know that this beautiful soul is protected by a great deal of light despite an unwise decision. This individual is not a lost soul or a condemned spirit. These are children of God who are treated with love, respect and compassion. Souls who have abandoned life are often hardest on themselves because the realization of their mistake is almost immediate. Feeling the pain of those left behind or seeing the faces of their unborn children is more haunting than whatever haunted them in life.

If you are in the depths of despair, reach out for help—now. It will always be given. You are so loved. And your immediate circumstances and current difficulties are temporary. With a little courage, you can and will begin to work and live in the light. Angels wait to assist you, but you must ask for help before intervention can occur.

Healing Visualization

1) Begin by thanking the universe for its love and support. Relax your body with ten deep breaths. Once your breathing is deep and even, picture yourself lying down with a magnetic block held above you. Starting at your feet, feel the block move up the length of your body, drawing up anything dark, cloudy or gray in your energy field.

2) When the magnet reaches the top of your head, see yourself standing up. Take the energy-cluttered block in hand. Release it up and out. See a golden light illuminate the sky, catching the block in its rays—liquefying it into gold.

3) Open your arms now. Allow your body to soak up pure healing energy like a sponge. Affirm that your body is perfect and whole.

Ask Spirit if there is anything else you need to do right now to facilitate healing. Listen to the voice within. When you feel at peace, thank the universe for its support. Pledge to keep your thoughts in light as you move through the day.

Chapter III
Love and Money

▼

The perfect love connection starts with love of self. If you do not honor and love yourself, you will attract people who do not honor and love themselves, either. They will mirror back to you feelings of worthlessness, lack of self-respect and estrangement from Spirit.

Think about your first experience as an adult in a love relationship. Most of us do not wish to return to the person we were, or to those we loved, in our early 20s. That's because our love of self was not as rich as it is today—and we attracted mates accordingly. This is not to say earlier relationships were not valuable experiences. They were, precisely because they provided the tools to expand our definition of love and partnership.

Inside Job

"What do I want and expect from love?" Once you get clear on that truth, you will attract the highest possible love. If, however, you get stuck in failing to realize you are glorious, you will continue to attract prospects who are less than glorious themselves. You need to honor yourself. Then affirm you will be in a relationship with someone who reflects that self-love back to you. Settle for nothing less. The universe will provide.

Attracting the best kind of partnership also means giving yourself some time off from the pursuit of love. Use the downtime to review old relationships. Make assessments you normally would not consider during this period of self-reflection. For example, instead of listing the negative things in a former relationship you do not wish to repeat, list all the good you do wish to repeat.

Although this may seem awkward initially, it's important to remember that you attracted all former relationships not simply to conclude that Mr. X or Ms. X was a dud. There was a moment, however fleeting, that each of your past relationships honored God.

Where was God honored? If you had children together, the answer is clear. Other relationships may require more introspection. Look for the kernel of love in each relationship that you previously remembered as dark. In this reframing of memories, you are literally creating new ones, which in turn lightens your load. Now you're storing memories at a cellular level that are of a higher order.

Quick, think of your worst relationship. See how quickly you dismiss it with, "Was I naïve" or (worse) "I certainly learned a lot from that one."

Again, are you telling the universe that pain helped you grow? Change the dialogue. Don't dismiss the old emotions, but reinspect and reconclude. Then ask yourself where God lives in the people you used to love. You may be surprised at the little sparks of light buried beneath your bleakest memories.

When you can capture some of the sacred essences that old relationships brought to bear, you are clearing the past. Any residual negativity, or experiences locked in a lower vibration, are forever transformed. You prepare your heart not just for new love, but spectacular love.

Most people are not aware they hold themselves back by thinking less than positively about former relationships—be they with family, friends or loved ones. We do. Thoughts not anchored in love vibrate at a lower level. Future relationships are drawn in accordingly.

If you can't identify love, what other soul quality developed from a given relationship? Perhaps strength was the byproduct of an unhappy home life. If you were in a situation where family love did not thrive, were you at least surrounded by the love of a teacher or friend? If so, thank God for that gift—and let the other less than perfect relationships fall away. By not being validated or supported by people who should have done so, you probably learned to validate and support yourself.

Just be careful how you frame that lesson. Many times people say, "I'm glad I went through all that I did; it made me who I am today." Again, rephrase. Unless you'd like to attract similar painful experiences in the future, draw a different conclusion. "I *chose* pain and lack to remind me that I am light and I am God. Now I remember. From this day forward I choose to experience my spirit through joy and abundance *only*."

Perhaps the soul quality of clarity emerged from a broken romance. Maybe sacred love was not what the universe was providing in terms of that life experience. Yet the insight you gained—about what is or is not important in a partnership—is what allows you to draw in a more profound love down the line. Without that clarity, it may have taken much longer to attract the loving and positive relationship the universe was (or is) eager to bring you.

Transform former relationships in your memory then. Bless them for the gifts they gave you. Then give the universe something specific to work with for the future.

> *When you capture some of the sacred essences*
> *that old relationships brought to bear, you are clearing the*
> *past. You are preparing your heart not just for*
> *new love, but spectacular love.*

What kind of relationship do you want? Some people crave high-intensity love. These souls desire the wild swings from together "as one" to painful separations, and back again. The highs are so intoxicating that stability is willingly sacrificed in this kind of coupling.

Other souls want a partner who values privacy or prefers a quiet homestead. There is no right or wrong answer here. Decide what you want. Affirm that the universe will provide that or something better. Then write it down.

List physical preferences, too. The physical component is important—not the least of which is for propagation of the species—but also because a strong physical bond allows you to connect with "all channels open" to the person you love. This is a much deeper connection than being with someone for whom you have deep affection without the physical attraction. When you connect with all channels open, there is the potential to recreate God in every intimate moment. It may not always occur, but the potential exists for God exaltation through intimacy.

If love exchange is not your intent, be aware that any merging of physical bodies changes your energy field forever. It's easy to absorb scattered and unwanted energy from the person with whom you are intimately engaged. Victims of sexual abuse are particularly vulnerable. Murky, weighty, negative energy from nonconsensual sexual contact wreaks havoc on every level. Like every imbalance or dis-ease, the disruption first appears in the aura, then manifests in physical form. Thus there's a tendency for sexual abuse victims to gain weight, not just as a means of self-protection from unwanted advances, but because the body mirrors what the heavy energy field already shows.

The glory of sexuality should never be taken lightly. While every sexual encounter need not be spiritual in nature, wisdom dictates that we use our bodies as a gift—as a sharing experience with others of a deep and profound love. If you cannot offer this gift, and instead are using your body as an instrument of power or release, be aware that you are tainting not only your partner's energy but also your own. Teach your children well: There is much more to the notion of sexual responsibility than protecting against unwanted conception.

When you decide what you need from a relationship—not to mention what you are prepared to give—you send the universe a very clear signal. How does this relationship make you feel? How does it make your partner feel? What is it that you—as a couple—contribute to the world? This final consideration is the most important. We are here individually and collectively to make a contribution to mankind and our fellow earth inhabitants. Your force as a couple stands in testament to that.

Once you start to ponder these questions, you cast about for the highest possible love. Patience is the key. Relationships happen when we least expect it. That's because there is no attachment involved. As soon as it becomes a "must have," fear takes root, repelling the very thing we want.

Find joy in everything else you do in the meantime. Focus on your job; praise God for the good things there. Be of service to others; volunteer. It takes the emphasis off you and creates a giving space in your heart. Above all, relax. Allow the universe to add bliss in the form of a partner when the timing is for the highest good of all concerned.

Most coupling, at least in the Western world, starts with the lure of eroticism. It is a compelling and magnificent force that holds sway with human beings of all ages.

As Eva Pierrakos discusses in *The Pathwork of Self Transformation* it is what drives even the most guarded personality to want to link in utmost intimacy with another soul. Yet the rush of falling into another person's energy is so powerful, it's easy to become distracted from its real intent: Love.

The drama and adrenaline surge that comes from initial attraction should be celebrated as a means to an end. If attraction is the icing (our first taste of sweetness) the cake— the substance of the dessert—is self-revelation to another or love. Eat just the icing and something's missing. Eat the cake and the icing, and you have a soul satisfying combination.

When you connect with all channels open, there
is the potential to recreate God in every intimate moment.
It may not always occur, but the potential exists
for God exaltation through intimacy.

The problem arises in long term relationships when the cake is stale and pretty much picked over! Therein lies the challenge. If you want to sustain a long term relationship with someone you love, discover new horizons on an otherwise familiar landscape. In other words, the relationship stays alive only insofar as you commit to discover the new, both in yourself and your loved one.

Says Pierrakos, "(The soul) has the capacity to reveal even deeper layers that already exist…the soul is endless and eternal: A whole lifetime would not suffice to know it."

As long as you and your partner are committed to revealing layers of yourself and growing together, the spark stays alive. The vibration between you stays charged.

External circumstances often provide the foundation for this energy exchange. Think of the mother who goes back to school to get her law degree, or the father who pursues his lifelong dream of car racing.

By seeking their own separate paths of joy, the other partner can't help but respond with awareness and intrigue. We find a similar sentiment echoed in Kahlil Gibran's *The Prophet,* "Love one another, but make not a bond of love: Let it rather be a moving sea between the shores of your souls…Let there be spaces in your togetherness, And let the winds of the heavens dance between you."

In some cases, a change in the status quo may at first be perceived as a threat or abandonment by the other person—at least at the personality level. But assuming a fair amount of emotional maturity in both partners, this is a win-win situation. Both people are actively engaged in peeling back and revealing new layers of themselves to each other, keeping the energy exchange alive.

If it does not feel joyful to continue your life journey with your partner, reinspect the relationship. You should never abandon a relationship in haste but neither should you hold on for dear life. If you have outgrown each other and would be better served taking the journey apart, the universe will signal you accordingly.

Never hold on to a relationship that has lost its life force. When you do, you lose yourself. You become captive to an idealized dream of what was or what you hoped would be. There is a much more magnificent reality awaiting you when you release. Remember the person you dated (or married) thirty, twenty or even ten years ago? That should verify, once again, that the universe will never take away from you without presenting something better.

And maybe that something better is yourself. You may be alone for two days or two decades. Make the most of it. Appreciate yourself, give love to others and get your life in order—especially your spiritual life...so that one day you will attract the utmost soul-satisfying love.

There is not just one soul mate in a lifetime. There are many types of loves that will flow in and out of your life. It depends on where you are spiritually and what you need to more fully manifest as your higher self at any given time. Stay open. Trust the universe to bring you exactly who you need, at exactly the right time.

The Richness in You

Money—the other big issue—is just one more external manifestation of internal dialogue and emotion. If you believe that you must struggle in order to create material wealth, the universe will teach you as you wish to be taught. On the other hand, if you affirm that your material growth occurs with a great deal of joy, your outer circumstances will likewise unfold.

The problem with money is essentially twofold: attachment and timing.

Fear-based attachment presents the universe with a real problem in manifesting for you. That's why it's important to affirm that you have everything you need in this moment, even if that's not your reality.

When the voice inside says, "yes, but I can't pay the electric bill" acknowledge the fear. After all, you created the situation to move dark into light. You also make the choice about how long you want those fear-based thoughts to linger.

> *The problem with money is essentially twofold:*
> *attachment and timing.*

New circumstances will unfold for you only when you shift your present perceptions. Creating a new reality out of anxiety does not work. Expecting to have peace externally when your inner world is in chaos is unrealistic.

Let's say you are confronted with an emergency car repair bill—and now you can't pay your rent. Ask yourself what you can do *right now* for your physical body to feel calm. Listen to the voice within. You may be urged to go for a walk. You may feel the need to nap or eat a nutritious meal. Do whatever feels like less of a struggle under the circumstances. There is a solution here. And the universe will challenge you to find one quickly.

When your anxiety level has subsided, sit down in a comfortable chair with pen and paper in hand. Take ten deep breaths. Ask yourself what this particular financial circumstance is teaching you.

Do you need to restructure or eliminate items in your monthly budget? Sometimes the lesson is less is more. Preoccupying one's self with material gain is never the answer if it takes you away from connecting with others at a soul level.

How has your money predicament brought you closer to Spirit? What of God have you remembered about yourself as a result of the lack of money?

Crises—financial or otherwise—are always a self-created effort to jump-start us back to the core of who we are. This does not have to be a mind-boggling exercise. You know the truth. As soon as you acknowledge it, you prepare for a different future.

If you are confronted with the same money problem over and over again, ask yourself what an abundant person would do in a similar situation. Put a face on the individual. Richard Branson, president of Virgin Atlantic, often comes to mind for me. That's because there is joy in everything he does—whether ballooning, sky diving or planning for a hotel in space.

Prosperous people tend to share common beliefs about self, so pick anyone you feel comfortable imagining. Then focus on these truths:

- An abundant person knows the universe is safe and generous.

- An abundant person does not "act from lack."

- An abundant person knows that bounty is our birthright; struggle is not necessary to achieve a rich and prosperous environment.

- An abundant person holds money problems lightly with a quiet knowledge that resolution will occur.

Allow yourself to adopt a similar mindset. Commit to viewing your financial affairs through the eyes of an abundant person. Then plan a winning strategy.

First, stop complaining about your bills. Instead tell everyone how lucky and appreciative you are for what you have. People will hold this "lucky" image of you in their minds, which energizes the new image you have of yourself.

Second, become more aware of how the manmade laws of finance operate. Interest rates, CDs, treasury bonds, stocks and mutual funds…these should become your new areas of expertise. If you take an ad hoc approach to money, it's no different than anything else in life: The results will be ad hoc, in constant flux, beyond your control. You probably would not take a hands-off approach to your career or child rearing, so do not take a hands-off approach to finances, either.

Next, write down the various essences money would give you if you did have a windfall of cash. Security, freedom, beauty…these are all essences that money can provide, but money does not have to be the only way for the universe to give them to you.

Introspection is the key. If you think money would give you the freedom to vacation, dig deeper. And the vacation would give you…what? Relaxation, stimulation? Once you've ascertained the core essence your soul is craving, you send a very clear signal for the universe to give exactly that to you. No one wants money just for the sake of being able to hold a wad of cash. It is the essence money provides that keeps us focused on achieving abundance.

You don't see a cook create a wonderful batter, then open the oven door every five minutes to take stock of the progress.

And as Duane Packer and Sanaya Roman note in their book *Creating Money*, often that essence will be presented before the material good. Here's an example.

Let's say a young man is hoping for a new car, specifically a cream-colored Mercedes. What the car represents for him is safety, status and security. This is what the man wants in his life right now, and he is focusing on a luxury car fulfilling these desires.

The essence of safety manifested first. The man received a small bonus at work and spent the money making repairs on his current vehicle. Suddenly he had a better feeling about driving his older car, and no longer worried about using the car on long business trips.

Status manifested two months later in a job promotion. Always a dedicated employee, the man accepted regional responsibilities for the marketing company where he was employed. Feeling that he had accomplished important work goals, he turned his attention to security—emotional security. The job shift was exactly what the young man needed to take his two year relationship with his girlfriend to a new level. He and his fiancee were married eight months later.

What about the Mercedes? He never did get the Mercedes. He did, however, buy a beautiful cream-colored Volvo a year into the marriage when he discovered his wife was expecting a baby.

Isn't it interesting how God gives us even better than we could have hoped, if we just stay open to receive? If this man had stayed attached to the notion of "I must have a Mercedes," instead of going with the flow, his inflexibility would have made it difficult for the universe to give him the essence of everything he wanted—and a life that exceeded his dreams.

Stay open and stay positive. Then release your goals to the universe. *Wait*, without despair, for your dreams to materialize. Unlike "in heaven" or however you wish to characterize the nonphysical world, thought does not automatically reproduce on the earth plane. And that's really a beautiful thing. Because if every thought manifested instantly, you would be extremely confused.

The real beauty lies in the actual creating of what you want. You've probably heard this before. There *is* God in the process. And God in the process is you harnessing your own energy to cocreate with Spirit. It's a rush. When you're in the higher flow, you experience the power of yourself. The old adage of, "half the fun is getting there" could not be more accurate. So expect a lag time. And do not undo your projections with worry.

One of the biggest mistakes people make is saying, "I've done all my affirmations. I've visualized until the cows come home, but still nothing. Maybe my life is never going to change."

The problem with this kind of thinking is that the worrying—translation: fear—about the desired result starts to mess up the seeds you've planted. All the positive input you've put into cultivating a strong and healthy dream garden begins to unravel. Would you plant a flower seed, then dig it up three days later to see what it's doing?

You don't see a cook create a wonderful batter, then open the oven door every five minutes to take stock of the progress. "It's a little brown over here. Is it sloping? It's never going to bake right." Yet when it comes to our own lives, how many times do we sabotage ourselves before we've given the universe half a chance to produce what we want?

The people who attract the things they desire are the ones who take a laissez faire attitude. Yes, they are clear on their wishes. But it is a quiet confidence that the universe will give them that, or something better, *at the perfect time*. This quiet confidence allows them to release that grasping "must have," fear-based disposition. Meanwhile they get on with the rest of their life with enthusiasm.

Does this mean they will manifest their dreams faster than someone with less confidence? Yes, because they are not undoing the initial request with anxiety and worry. But—and here's the caveat—not always as quickly as *they* would like, either. And that's because to everything there is a season.

You may affirm and visualize with quiet confidence for long stretches of time—or for a very short period of time—before your request manifests. It will manifest when the timing is perfect for *you*. You will never be presented with anything you are not ready to receive at every level: mental, physical and emotional.

When you do receive it, of course, it's up to you how to embrace it. You can take your accomplishment to a higher level and use it to add more light to the world—or not. But the dream, in its most basic state, will not unfold for you until it is for your highest good and the highest good of those it will impact in its most preliminary form.

Plant your seeds with enthusiasm and love. Release your hopes for fruition—gently. Then let the earth work its magic.

Light Infusion

What if your fear is so pervasive you cannot break the cycle of continually pushing away what you want?

If you spend most of your day plagued with despair about everything that is missing from your life—including love or money—there is a problem. Know that your entire body, right down to your cells, is resonating with thoughts of lack. Your vibration or "tone" is merely an amplification of these beliefs, which in turn draws in more experiences of the same. You're caught in a vicious circle.

> *Watch the old tape. Someone else's truth*
> *does not have to be your truth. Whose words*
> *are holding you hostage?*

Check your internal dialogue. What you say to yourself can sabotage your best efforts no matter how confident

you try to be about your finances, relationships or anything else. Watch the old tape. Someone else's truth does
not have to be your truth. Whose words are holding you
hostage? If you pig out under stress, rack up endless debt,
or abuse drugs and alcohol, what tape in your head keeps
sabotaging your best intentions?

Words from adults, particularly when we're small, last.
You may be trying hard to attract money or enjoy a loving
relationship with someone who honors you, but the internal dialogue nails you every time. If you're still listening to
tapes of "you're stupid," "you're fat," "no one likes you,"
"you're ugly," "you'll never amount to anything," it's time
to take stock of how and why these words came to be.

It's one thing to hear these words from our peers; it's
another if they come from our caretakers. Because a
child is so enmeshed with a parental figure—in even the
most abusive of situations—words are taken to heart
and internalized.

The truth of the matter is the adult is likely repeating
what was said to him or her as a child. The parent then
perpetuates that cycle by repeating the same words, and
projecting their own fears of inadequacy, onto their
offspring.

Unfortunately a child or teenager doesn't have the cog-
nitive skills to discern this familial dynamic. So the child
internalizes there is something wrong with him.

Stop right now and take back your power. Recognize
any situation you've already lived through for what it was.
Do not carry someone's else's burden. It is not yours to
bear. Forgive the person if you can. Recognize the fundamental fact that they, too, operated from the principle of
spiritual growth through pain.

You may not have received the kind of love you needed. This is not a reflection of your worthiness; it is a reflection of someone else's inner tapes. Grieve for what you lost. Then reparent yourself. You absolutely have enough love within you to do so.

If the people who hurt you are still alive, lower your expectations. They may never self-reflect or take responsibility. That's okay. You can thrive without validation. Don't wait for someone else to give that to you. It won't come until people are ready to do the hard and dirty work, and that may never occur.

> *Spirit is waiting to give you your heart's desires. But first you must understand you are worthy to receive.*

Have you forgotten? *You are a child of God, before you are anybody else's child!* You are loved and adored and perfect. Spirit is waiting to give you your heart's desires. But first you must understand you are worthy to receive. If you don't believe it, settle in God's arms for awhile. Reestablish your balance. Then ask that your body become a receptacle for light. Request that the restorative power of the universe come to and through you.

- Picture yourself lying down with a soft wave of light coming toward you. Inhale.

- As the wave washes over your body, feel each of your cells opening to and receiving this light. Exhale.

- Repeat this several times. When you feel peaceful, and your breathing is deep and even, mentally affirm: "All my fears gently wash away. I am healed and whole."

• Now see yourself in a scene—exactly as you wish to be. If your desire is to be in a relationship, feel yourself merging with a kindred soul who loves you. If you want more money, envision yourself in the surroundings that money will buy. Feel the joy. Thank the universe. Gently release the image.

As your cells respond to the light in this exercise, you may receive mental symbols of new beginnings—buds sprouting, birds hatching. Or you may sense nothing but peace. Either way, focus with gratitude on the very nucleus of your cell being penetrated by the light.

After the exercise has run its course—when it starts to feel heavy to continue—stop. Thank Spirit for the support and love. Begin your day or drift off to sleep.

You have just programmed yourself anew. By filling yourself with the highest energies of light and love, your vibration is returning to its natural unimpeded state. Your cells are transformed.

Throughout the day, you must make a conscious effort to watch your thoughts. Anything you focus on for more than 15 seconds impacts your vibration. So if you find yourself reverting to old thought patterns, stop. Turn your attention back to yourself. Place your hand over your heart. Repeat silently, "I love myself. All my dreams manifest in the perfect time. Thank you Universe. I grow through joy."

You *are* in the process of recreating your life. Patience is the key. Remember: Even people who release their desires with quiet confidence will not manifest those dreams until the timing is perfect for them. There is a time for harvest and there is a time for fallow periods. The beauty of the seasons is that jubilance is always yours for the asking; each season simply adds a different hue to life's experiences.

During a fallow period you may feel an urge to stay focused on family, and find your joy there. During a period of bounty you may find yourself extroverted, and eager to share the fruits of your labor with the world. There need not be struggle in either period, simply a refocusing of energies and a commitment to live in the higher flow regardless.

As always, one slight shift in your belief about self, and the universe will begin to reflect that new reality back to you: in every area, including love and money.

Chapter IV
Magnetizing

▼

What brings you closest to God? You know what it is. It's a rush; it's your joy flood. When my daughter laughs, this is a joy flood. Nothing compares. Time stands still. My life is perfect. When I look into the eyes of any animal, my heart is flooded with joy. I am one with God.

Many of us are so busy doing, we forget to just be. It's difficult to find the time to fill our lives with pleasurable things, let alone slow down enough to relish whatever brings us true joy.

If your household is being dictated by the need to stay on the fast track, reconsider your options. If spending more time with your family would fill your hours with happiness, change your lifestyle. And remember, material gain and spiritual joy are not mutually exclusive. You don't have to give up your Lexus to have inner peace.

Abundance is ours for the asking. If this car, that house, or this set of jewelry fills you with bliss, you shall have them. The caveat is if you feel you must have them, and then work to support the material gain at the expense of your spiritual life, you will be thrown off balance. And the universe will signal you accordingly.

Material gain and spiritual joy are not mutually exclusive.

What *does* give you joy? If you don't know, this exercise may help. Many spiritual teachers have used this—or something similar—to help students pinpoint the life their soul is craving. Pretend that money is no object, and you do not have any responsibilities other than to yourself.

Your Perfect Day

•   What time is it when you wake up? What does your bed look and feel like? Is anyone lying beside you? Is it rainy and cozy, or is it bright and sunny when you open your eyes?

•   What would give you maximum pleasure as you step out of bed? Perhaps you need a moment to meditate or a cup of strong coffee and the newspaper. Maybe you'd enjoy a walk in your garden. Money and your day-to-day responsibilities are not an issue here. So if you have three kids under the age of five and you're thinking "yeah, like I have a choice," they are with a loving caregiver in this fantasy. This time is for you.

•   How do you want to spend the rest of your day? Break it down into two or three hour increments. Some people get a joy rush in the business world. They light up at the office, whether they need the money or not. Other souls prefer a more solitary environment—constructing crafts or reading a book. Perhaps you crave high level physical activities: a workout at the gym, basketball or a game of golf. Whether you choose fishing, wood carving or stock market trading, you will find yourself gravitating to an activity where time passes unnoticed for you. When you lose a sense of time it is a true indication of being in the higher flow.

- As the day unwinds, how do you want it to end? If you live in Kansas and your ideal day concludes with a walk on the beach, that's fine. Visualize the experience that brings you the utmost joy regardless of where you are right now. Some people may need a high energy cocktail party or the equivalent of a night on the town to unwind. You may prefer a bubble bath and soft music. Whatever your ideal day looks like—and however it ends— record it on paper.

The reason it is important to write the information is twofold. First, thoughts are things. When you couple an idea with the physical act of writing, you infuse that thought with a huge dose of energy before it travels out to the universe. Your imagination (thought) is working in conjunction with your physical body (the act of writing) and the power increases exponentially.

Anything that starts with joy, which is a demonstration of love for yourself, is by its very nature the sturdiest of foundations. The universe will work very hard to create exactly what you've asked for. You will not have to struggle to get it. Your life may be in total disarray, but if you do this exercise with the intent to create your own slice of heaven on earth, how could you be denied?

God, Spirit, the universal energy wants for you exactly what you want for yourself and more. Trust. Listen to the voice within. And start to take small practical steps to reshape your day.

If you are waking up to chaos, this is the first area of your life that needs to be revised. A day of joy, any kind of joy, needs to begin with peace. That sets the tone—not to mention the vibration you take with you into the world. If you start with chaos, more chaos is sure to follow.

Change what happens when you first get out of bed. It may mean getting more done the night before; it may mean asking for and receiving more help from your children or spouse.

You are in control as much as you allow yourself to be. If you start the day resonating an inner calm, other family members will be soothed by your presence. This does not mean your children will suddenly become angels, but it does mean the energy of the house will shift when even one person starts the day centered.

"Peaceful" and "centered" is going to mean something different for everyone. Some people will achieve that state through meditation. Others will want to work out. Still others will sound their brightest note only after a look at the sports page. If there is one common denominator, it is that the focus must be on *you* at the very beginning of each day.

If the bulk of your day is spent trying to make money to pay the bills, this is the next area of your life that needs a major overhaul. Look at your perfect day. Look at your current day. What activities are missing? Can you make money with those activities?

Once you commit to pursue your passions, the universe will give you more support than you could imagine. If, however, you continue to deny what your soul wants, Spirit will make it increasingly difficult for you to engage in the status quo.

The universe will work very hard to create your perfect day. You will not have to struggle to achieve what brings you joy.

Start planning now for a job transition if you are not doing your life's work. How do you know what your life's work is? Look at your passions at age 11 or 12. Reflect on times in your life when you felt in synchronization with the universe. They may be only fleeting moments—perhaps they even occurred in your teens or 20s—but it is in those moments that your soul light shined.

What will your obituary list as your accomplishments? This may seem like a morbid consideration, but consider it anyway. Your life could end tomorrow. Have you wasted your time? Wouldn't it be sad to leave this earth when you have not even tried to leave something of value behind?

Like everyone else I have been guilty of the, "When I get this, I will do that." Neale Donald Walsch says it so beautifully in *Conversations with God, Book I*, "Fake it till you make it." As you work on those inner adjustments, live the life of your dreams.

If you plan to do volunteer work once you can easily pay your bills, do the volunteer work first. The rest of your life will immediately move to an elevated state to match your selfless deeds.

If you want to be slim, pretend you already have a body to die for. Dress up; look exquisite. If you want to be rich, do what a rich person would do, even if it is once a month: have lunch at the most expensive restaurant in town; learn another language; plan a trip to Europe.

This tells the universe you have new beliefs about self: I am giving, I am prosperous, I am beautiful. The universe supports these beliefs by creating more experiences of the same. Keep it in perspective, though. Fun experiences for the personality do not satisfy the soul unless they are grounded in love and reverence for life.

Whenever I daydream about traveling to exotic locations "in the future," I remind myself I can have the essence of that experience right now, in our own backyard. (And it's going to be a lot more fun than taking a small child on a plane.) Exotic food, music and a little creativity come close to recreating the ambiance of any locale. The best part: We can have friends and family there, which would not be possible with the real deal.

I do not have to wait until money is plentiful or my baby is the right age to enjoy traveling. I can take the essence of any place my soul is craving and make it real at home.

Do not postpone your life until you're richer, smarter, saner or whatever it is you think you're missing! Be what you want to be, and where you want to be, now—even if it is not an objective truth.

Tell the universe what brings you joy. The universe is your biggest supporter and your number one ally. No request is too trivial, no request is too monumental to fulfill. If it resides in light, trust the universe to provide that or something better. And be sure to say thank you when it arrives.

The misconception is we think we can effect change in our life in one of two ways. Either we do it all on our own. Or God hands us everything we want on a silver platter. The truth: The universe is waiting for you to step up to the plate. God wants you as a partner.

If you do it on your own, you're missing the element of divinity. If you hand it over to God, you're abdicating your responsibility as co-constructor of your time on earth. Either way it's an impediment to soul full living. Work together with Spirit. That is your way back to the higher flow.

The misconception is we think we can effect change in our life in one of two ways. Either we do it on our own. Or God hands us everything we want on a silver platter.

And what is so great about the often-mentioned higher flow? The lack of struggle. Consider the rip tide as an example. You're swimming in the ocean and suddenly the current shifts. You find yourself pushed farther from shore. Panic sets in. You struggle to get back the same way you came. Big mistake. Because now you're swimming against the current. And swimming against the current creates more fear, panic and struggle.

How dissimilar is this from life? When presented with challenges, many of us let abject fear dictate our responses rather than trust God has a better way. Which begs the question, is God really with me? If so, why put me in the middle of the rip tide in the first place?

If God is by my side, why does my car break down when I barely have enough money to meet my monthly expenses? Why do I keep dating losers? God is with you. And the fact that you are able to choose ease as a means of navigation—as opposed to struggle—is your soul's and God's gift to you.

You can swim against the current in an attempt to get back to the point of origin. Your body will tire. Panic will ensue. Or you can calm yourself and ask for assistance in reaching the higher flow.

Going with the flow literally propels you back to safety. Swimming with the current, parallel to the shore in the case of the rip tide, sets you free. How different is this from life? We can take the hard way or the easy way. Take the path of least resistance if you want to grow through joy. Stay where you are or push against the current, and the universe will see that you get back to Spirit…through struggle.

Most of us are quick to say what we do not want in this life. "I do not want to get caught in a rip tide, tangled in seaweed or eaten by a shark when all I'm trying to do is enjoy a day at the beach." Okay.

Now reframe the description. Tell the universe what you do want. Hold the highest possible vision for yourself. Commit to incorporate your soul's desire to love in every aspect of your life.

When you are prepared to enjoy life as pure Spirit, coming from the highest organizing principle of the universe—love—you will find yourself creating far fewer rip tides in your day-to-day affairs.

Shine as an Example

Helping and loving others is the only thing that matters when all is said and done. If you are drawn to this book and the information resonates as truth for you, this is an important lifetime for you to make a contribution to the world.

Work through the fear and anger in your own life first. People on a spiritual path often think it is noble to turn away from areas of their life that are not light. In turning away, you deny the potential for excellence and transformation on a huge scale.

Have you heard the expression that your greatest liability has in it the seeds to become your greatest asset? The albatross around your neck, the issues you cannot seem to conquer, are the very same ones that can give you your salvation and possibly lead to the salvation of others.

Besides, whatever you deny only becomes stronger.

Let's say you committed a crime. The truth is too hard to accept. So you bury the information and proceed to get on with life. Whatever you repress, so too you express…to the universe at large this time. Some of the negativity will get trapped in your physical body with the potential to cause ailments there. The rest of the energy, unless spoken of, written of, or otherwise acknowledged, will float out to the universe and actually gather more power. The deed, in effect, attracts more energy of the same. Other thoughts and actions set at the same tone vibrate with your crime, magnifying the original act. This is how some people literally create their own living hell.

Contrast this with the potential to direct fear-based energy into energy of a higher order. Once emotion is expressed with the intent of *healing* a situation, there is a shift. The person suffering from the shame—or guilt—of the original crime is automatically released from the self-created prison. And there is now the potential to use that experience to enlighten others.

> *The albatross around your neck, the issues you cannot seem to conquer, are the very ones that can give you your salvation—and possibly lead to the salvation of others.*

The flip side is interesting, too. Positive thoughts, dreams and wishes will gather more power if unexpressed. If you decide you want something in life…hush. Gently detach and keep quiet. Let your inner desires gather power from other likeminded thoughts floating in the universe. That way your wish is able to gather momentum, unimpeded, in the higher realms.

If you speak of your heart's desires, some people may denigrate the viability of your dreams. On the one hand, this acts as a good mirror for any self-doubts you may harbor. It allows you to confront and heal your fears when others act in a nonsupportive way. The problem is the lower thoughts of others can also attach themselves to your dreams, slowing your progress. Best to use the laws of the universe to know that what remains in secret gathers power.

When you have done sufficient clearing of your own issues, don't forget to give back to the world. Shine as an example to others. Ask to serve. God will use you and your unique gifts to spread light and effect positive change. Do not demand to know exactly how. Just ask to be a vehicle for Spirit to maximize healing and fortify the human race with love and forgiveness.

And we have so much to forgive each other for! We are all God's children. The pain we inflict on others due to illusory differences is almost unbearable. Every nasty thought or painful aside tears the fabric that binds us. Angels weep at our cruelty, to each other, to animals, to the environment. And yet the naysayers have it wrong. There is no world end, but rather world transformation. It is our blueprint to create heaven on earth. God did not create us to destroy ourselves. God created us and then encouraged us to experience ourselves as masters of physicality—as human beings expressing Godliness through a body. How long it takes each of us to awaken to our individual power, and how often we fall down in the process, is up to us.

In the meantime, we learn what we do and do not want as a human race. Military skirmishes and terrorist activities show us the light. They create in us a need to reverse course, to heal. "This we want, this we do not want" is the clarity they provide. And every time we heal on a personal level, by dealing with our own internal demons, we add one more healing dimension to mass consciousness.

You cannot stop the light. That's why the last few years have been so transformational for many of us. Depending on how much of a Shakespearean tragedy you've agreed to star in, you may have lost everything in order to more fully embrace who you are.

If you have been pushed to shed an old skin, rejoice. The universe is preparing you to move more fully into a light body that allows you to get up and glow. You may not feel like an example to others, yet. But as you learn to swim the joyful stream, that's the course that will inspire—not only your life, but the lives of those you come in contact with daily.

There are plenty of prognosticators who predict the end of the world. California will fall into the ocean, nuclear holocaust will end the world...we've heard them all. If you believe strongly enough that the world is going to come to a violent end, you will find yourself positioned in areas of the world where violent undertakings can occur.

You cannot help but resonate with energy of a similar nature. So if you're just positive that floods or fires, earthquakes or lava flow will consume the world, then guess what? You will find yourself drawn to areas where there is a greater potential for this type of disaster.

From a different perspective, there is so much light transforming the world right now that the old can't help but accede to the new. There is literally a shaking off of coarse energy as the earth prepares for a more harmonious future.

> *God created us and then encouraged us to experience ourselves as masters of physicality... as human beings expressing Godliness through a body.*

So to see weather changes and interpret them as disastrous is as regrettable as looking at the Northern Ireland peace accord and saying it will never work because extremists oppose it. Or an Israel/PLO breakthrough is not viable...end of story. Is the glass half empty or half full? Negotiators are sitting at the table. People are seeking a better way to live. Some souls may eschew the changes in favor of violence, discord and hate. But that is their reality and one that does not need to impact you, unless you expect it will.

As the rest of the world commits to joy, you will see the power of the disgruntled few fall away.

There are many light workers around the world committed to peace and tolerance. More souls awaken to their own power every day. Thank the universe for the strides made in AIDS and cancer research. Thank the universe for worldwide benefits that assist hungry children, and outreach programs that help the old and disabled. Thank the universe for broadening our understanding of the rights of animals and children. Be grateful you do not hold the same prejudicial views against minority groups as perhaps your parents or grandparents did. Are we where we need to be as a human race? No. But let's acknowledge progress and give ourselves credit where credit is due.

SECTION II

EXPANSION AND JOY

▼

It is now time to try softer. It is now time to be willing to let all the powers

and energies of the universe work for you. It is a time for you to be open…to

allow those energies to carry you to your next step. It is a time for joy.

—Ruth Fishel

CHAPTER V
POWER SURGE

▼

Do not give your power away. You've probably heard this before. If you want to live a life of joy, without struggle, you need to live this truth daily.

1) Do not give your power away to the people who love you. This may be the most difficult power play to execute because the natural inclination is to try and please your loved ones. Unfortunately, doing for others often means you do without. Put yourself first. When your tank is full—because you have honored your own needs—you can direct maximum energy not only to the people you love, but to wherever else you wish to spread light.

Two lovely ladies I know struggle to make ends meet. They are living on the brink of poverty. Both are in poor health. Together out of fear they have created an untenable situation for themselves.

The daughter is unable to set appropriate boundaries vis-a-vis the mother. The Mom is 88 and unwilling to go into a nursing home. She is dependent on her daughter for all social, financial and health needs. The daughter is bitter, even though she herself created the dynamics that allow the situation to continue. Rather than set up a life of her own, and then work her mother into it, the daughter has chosen to postpone almost all aspects of living until her mother passes away. And Mom isn't exactly on her deathbed, despite some chronic aches and pains.

This may be the most difficult power play to execute because the natural inclination is to try and please your loved ones.

Both of these beautiful women are lively and spirited. The octogenarian Mom longs for a boyfriend; the daughter longs for her freedom. Instead of living, however, they've woven themselves into a cocoon that does not allow either to breathe.

Most of us do not create familial situations this extreme for ourselves—where one's freedom is literally at stake. We do, however, regularly compromise ourselves in small ways to please and appease our loved ones.

Listen to the small voice within. Be aware of how your body reacts, even if you're asked to do something as minor as share a meal with someone who does not honor you. If you feel a tension in the pit of your stomach, but agree to go along to keep the peace, the universe will support you in your belief that you are not worthy of being honored by everyone.

This doesn't mean you should throw a tantrum—"I'm not going if X, Y and Z are there"—but it does mean you need to set comfortable limits, coming from a level of right action and self-respect. Once you do, your vibration will be infused with additional light. And you will attract the best in all aspects of your life.

2) Do not give away your power to someone you think has all the answers. The only person who has all the answers for you is you. People may inspire you. But as soon as you give your power to a teacher or healer, you are back to square one.

Heal yourself. Minister yourself. Ask the universe to provide support players in the form of doctors or spiritual counselors, but know that you are the star. The world is your stage. "In this world full of people, only some want to fly, isn't that crazy?" writes musician Seal. It's not that people don't want to fly; they've forgotten they have the power to do so. And we do have the power to do anything, at all times, because we are physical manifestations of God.

Reject anything that does not come from love. It is not for your highest good. When I was in my 20's and living in San Diego, I discovered a spiritual group that intrigued me. It was not a church, but rather a self-proclaimed "order." A successful female executive where I worked was a member, so I thought I'd check it out.

The information was interesting. There were discussions of spiritual growth, how to create abundance in your life and so on. It did strike me as odd, however, that the whole group functioned as a hierarchy. There were no equals there. You started out at the lowest level—sort of like a freshman at a fraternity or sorority—and moved up accordingly.

After a few group dinners and an initiation ceremony, I figured I could learn a lot from such a wise group…despite the less than egalitarian arrangement. I eagerly awaited hearing head honcho "Joey" speak.

When Joey spoke, people listened. Joey, however, had some peculiar habits. After the first night's lecture, he spent a lot of time patting women on their behinds. A few weeks later, at a group dinner, Joey walked up to me and casually pushed my elbows off the table. One of my sponsors told me it was an effort to "reinforce the notion of discipline." How weird is that? I thought. This guy is supposed to be Mr. Spirituality. I stuck with the group nonetheless.

When it came time for me to graduate to level 2, I had to memorize a spiritual poem to say in front of my two sponsors. I was a little nervous, but I stood up proud as a peacock ready to deliver.

"Oh, and take off your clothes," they announced. "What?" The room was dark and lit with candles. Suddenly I saw the absurdity of the whole situation! I knew it wasn't a sex thing, thank God. But it was your basic power thing.

"Take off your clothes; we need to strip down your pride."

Yeah…right. You've never seen anyone bolt faster. I hopped into my little brown Honda, practically drove through the property gate and I was outta there.

The moral of the story: If it does not come from love, it is not of the highest order. Stripping one's pride, humiliation, "starting at the bottom," deferring to a self-proclaimed authority on matters of your soul…these tactics are not born from love, but they do manifest as tools of ego.

I never had a good feeling about Mr. Joey or the group arrangement. I thought the information was interesting. I did not know the same information would manifest easily from other venues without the accompanying shenanigans.

Whether you are seeing a therapist, working with a spiritual group or tending to matters of your health, you should always feel an undercurrent of love in the environment. If you do not feel elevated by the encounter, look elsewhere. Any teacher's power should augment *your* power, not the other way around.

> *Stripping one's pride, humiliation, deferring to a self-proclaimed authority on matters of your soul... these tactics are not born from love, but they do manifest as tools of ego.*

Many healers, for example, are gifted souls. How is their personal manner? If their touch or conduct is devoid of love, you deserve better. Ask for a loving healer or teacher to come into your life. Then expect the interaction to be brief. Otherwise you run the risk of turning over your power.

The best healers manifest as a pure channel for Spirit. The ego is moved aside and the healer comes from a place of love for humanity. Does this mean you need to find an angel on earth in order to have a satisfying spiritual experience? No. The person you encounter may be ordinary, but when they heal or teach they operate from a place of love guided by the Holy Spirit.

That is their gift. You should feel empowered, not diminished, in their presence. You should feel supported, not criticized. You should not be lectured about religious conversion or hit up for donations. There are many different paths to God. But any that employ pressure as a means to an end are not of the highest order.

Several years ago I worked with a healer who let me agonize, lament and rage without wavering in her support. I was a fireball of negative energy—physically and psychologically. It would have been easy for her to get fed up and frustrated. (Or at the very least lecture me about what I was doing wrong with my life.) Never happened. Whenever there was a shift in my consciousness—whenever I let in a little more light—she never took credit. She simply declared that it was me healing myself. If I became too dependent, "oh, please can I schedule another healing session…like, tomorrow?" I was gently reminded not to give my power away. All totaled, we worked together about six months.

Your experience may be different. The teachers you attract may be with you for a slightly longer or shorter duration. Regardless of the time frame, it is always you who has all the answers. You are the greatest authority on you—not your priest, minister or therapist. They are only support players, albeit sometimes significant ones, on your journey to living the life of your dreams.

3) **Do not give your power away to karma.** "I must be broke all the time because I did something bad with money in a past life." Are you giving your power away to a concept, to unseen universal forces? Careful. If you think you must be punished for past deeds—in this life or others—the universe will fulfill this point of view no matter what joyful things you are doing with your life.

Usually we hope karma will unfold judiciously for other people, if not ourselves. How many times have we been hurt in a love relationship and then watch the perpetrator go on to a great relationship with someone new? We're waiting for the karma thing to kick in, but this person is living the life of Riley. And as far as we can tell, their life just keeps getting better and better. It probably is. This person likely did not plan to hurt you nor do they expect to be punished for hurting you. Thus they go on their merry way while we sit waiting to exclaim, "Yowsa, you finally got yours."

We pull in specific people to move us along to where we need to be. Should someone with whom you've had a difficult relationship be punished or applauded? This person gave you a gift very specific to your needs. They became a player in your drama and you in theirs. The slate was wiped clean when the relationship ended. You got what you needed, even if it was a bitter little pill, and they got what they needed. The karma is finished then and there. There is no deed that needs to be "balanced." That's why you rarely see the person who wronged you move into a dire situation as payback for what they did to you.

Then we say, "Oh, they'll get theirs when they die." That's dubious, too. Because if they were contributing to your higher good by acting in a particularly unpleasant way, is that good or bad?

When they leave this physical plane they will have the opportunity to review their life, including every thought and feeling you experienced in your interaction with them. They will make their own judgment about the kinds of seeds they planted. You, likewise, will have the same opportunity.

Start today to release the antiquated notion of karma. None of us needs or should expect to be punished for past interactions. None of us needs to incorporate pain into the equation of spiritual growth. As we create each new moment with every new thought, we are truly starting fresh.

We do not walk bound into the future, chained by our past thoughts and deeds—only by our beliefs. True, many souls will continue to feed into the belief that what goes around comes around. If, however, you look at your own experience, you will find that instant karmic moments are few and far between.

We pull in specific people to move us along to where we need to be. Should someone with whom you've had a difficult relationship be punished or applauded?

Look at Adolf Hitler. What is a more glaring example of evil intent? Yet the belief system of this individual allowed his intention to climax to outlandish proportions. The Final Solution and military assaults unfolded over more than half a decade—with very little "cause and effect" flowing back to Mr. Hitler. Was he not inwardly miserable, and did he not perish in some bunker in a particularly unpleasant way? To be sure. That, however, is hardly comparable to the pain and degradation this single human being inflicted on millions of innocent people. Where's the balance in that equation?

The mitigating factor is always one's belief system. Hitler's beliefs about Jews and ethnic cleansing, not to mention his tireless campaign to restore power to a beleaguered post-WWI Germany, fueled his rise to power and allowed him to create a heinous reality. He *believed* he was doing the right thing, and he convinced thousands of others to believe the same thing.

Anyone with a flicker of "belief" that maybe they were doing something wrong would have created a much different reality at some point along the way. Hitler never wavered, as anyone with a conscience would have.

Noted author M. Scott Peck says in his book *People of the Lie* that the most dangerous people on this earth are not those in prison, as we might otherwise think. On the contrary, a person in prison has demonstrated rather concretely to the universe their belief that they did something wrong. There is a conscience at work: That's why they've put themselves behind bars.

Souls that operate on the periphery of society—without reflection—are the ones who damage themselves and others with impunity. When a fundamental moral code is lacking in someone's psychological makeup there is no introspection. There is no empathy. And that person's belief system, however skewed, carries the day unchallenged until a new belief about self and any pain they've inflicted takes root.

Let's say my intent is to hurt you. If my belief is that you deserve to be hurt because you are a threat to my family—or however I frame it—and I am unwavering in my belief, the world around me remains largely unchanged even after I've hurt you.

My intent may be to love you. If my belief system is that with love comes pain, hurt and abandonment, then we all know what kind of reality I will create for myself— and it has nothing to do with intent.

Few parents start out with any other intention but to love their children. Yet we know that most families today operate with a significant amount of dysfunction. The intention did not create the dysfunction, the beliefs about self did.

Be careful what you project onto other people. If you subscribe to the notion that "hey, you took $10 from me, now someone's going to take $20 from you" you're making that operating principle real only for yourself. You're not making your view about karma real for the person who took $10 from you! That would have to come from their own *belief* that they did something wrong. And if they don't register they did—and if, in fact, they inadvertently taught you a lesson by acting as a mirror for your own beliefs about self (i.e., I'm always being robbed by other people)—who's to say the taking of the $10 is definitively a bad thing? What if, just to add another variable, the person who stole from you spent the money on medicine for their child?

In any case, the karma is cleared then and there. You drew that person to you and vice versa. Rejoice in the experience. And do not worry about anyone else's beliefs. What they believe about themselves—and their corresponding reality—is exactly where they need to be right now. The universe will gently move each of us towards a more joyful existence when we're ready to stop the struggle and surrender to the light.

If, however, your inner dialogue continues with: "Wow, it's during the dry times I really find out about myself," the invitation is for more pain to come into your life. Your belief system is what will keep taking you back to the struggle not the concept of karma.

Nothing happens without our soul's permission.
This is true not just of humans, but of all life forms.

What about when tragedy descends on someone's life seemingly out of the blue? Could that be karma at work? There are no accidents. When you see an innocent victim suffer a great mishap it often has more to do with volunteerism than cause and effect. The personality may not register this as truth at first. In fact, the "why me" response is generally what takes precedence at times of tragedy. Nobody thinks of themselves as having willingly agreed to have something bad happen to them. On a deep level, however, nothing happens without our soul's permission.

True, some souls may have made that choice out of a desire to grow—using the old model that only through great struggle comes great growth. Others, however, have simply agreed to take on a seemingly untenable situation to remind us of what is real and what is true in this world.

Rachel Scott, one of the first victims to die at Columbine High School, wrote in her diary: "Dear God, Please use me to reach the unreached." Followed by an entry in 1998: "This will be my last year, Lord. I've gotten all I can." Her father stumbled upon these diary entries after her death.

Nothing happens without our soul's permission. This is true not just of humans, but of all life forms. Animals are just as capable as human beings in shifting universal consciousness. Every life is connected. When an animal is abused, just as when a human being is abused, we are all affected and depleted spiritually until one act of kindness shifts our collective consciousness again.

There are many souls in the world putting their physical selves in danger for the greater good of humanity. Against the greatest odds, these souls teach the glory of Spirit. The rest of the world is inspired by their light as they show us how to turn our attention away from disease, disaster and lower vibrations to the sanctity of life.

That is one way of being of service to humanity, but it is not the only way. You do not need to suffer to learn and you do not need to suffer to teach. There is but one universal mind. The painful experiences of all those who have gone before you are always available for your contemplation and reflection.

Thank the universe for their courage and sacrifice. And remember how their suffering led us back to what we had forgotten in the first place: We are all connected in Love. Our hearts beat as one.

You do not need to suffer to learn and you do not need to suffer to teach. The painful experiences of those who have gone before you are always available for your contemplation and reflection.

Do not give your power away to old principles. If you want to experience yourself as Divine, restructure your beliefs about how to get there. All paths lead to God. And there is nothing of a karmic nature you need take with you as you walk with love into the future.

4) **Do not give your power away to unresolved issues.** If you're not where you want to be at this moment in time, be gentle with yourself. Old thought patterns take anywhere from 30 to 60 days to clear.

Concentrate now on which areas of your life need a joy infusion. Then open to receive love there. There is no such thing as too much happiness, unless you believe at some level you do not deserve it. Visualize and expect greatness. When you get a little, ask for more. You're not taking away from anyone in the process—in fact, the more you get for yourself, the more others realize they can have it all too.

When you first start living in and reaping the rewards of living a life of joy, you may be tempted to spread the gospel. Not a good idea. Do not disrupt someone else's status quo. They will release their pain when they are ready.

Seek and speak your truth. By all means. Relish your power surge. You will discover yourself making connections with new people, forging deeper and more meaningful bonds. The downside, although it's not really a downside, is that some of your old relationships will fall away.

If you discover you are losing things you had in common with friends and loved ones, gently detach. Let them be. Release with love. Before you do, though, put yourself in their shoes just for a moment—particularly if there are unresolved issues between you. It's a simple exercise, but most of us don't take the time to do it because we're so caught up in our own agenda.

Breathe deeply. Think of the person you are trying to understand. What do you know about their past? Integrate whatever you do know into your experience of seeing the world through their eyes. Imagine you are the other person in this conflict.

How does this situation appear to you? How does it feel for you? Honor whatever feelings or impressions you receive. This is what your soul wants you to know about this other person right now.

Performing this empathy exercise is important on many levels. First, it gives you a glimpse into the inner world of another. It's like putting on a pair of much needed prescription glasses to view a movie screen. "Oh, now I get it." You're seeing more of the complete picture. At the very least you should sense the other person's pain, which will add another dimension of understanding to your viewpoint.

Use this exercise to view all unresolved relationships. Ask your higher self if there is any incident you've experienced, from infancy on, that needs to be seen from another person's perspective.

John Bradshaw's book *Healing Your Inner Child* instructs readers to connect with each parent's inner child in order to appreciate the wounds our parents carry with them. You can perform a similar viewing with anyone in your life, not just your parents.

Ask to connect with that person's soul. What unresolved pain colors their behavior? How does it feel for them? Are they sorry? Are you ready to forgive them? If not, do not force yourself to forgive. Just sense what that person experienced in the situation and file it for future reference.

If you are ready to forgive, extend your forgiveness on the inner planes with love and compassion. It does not have to be complicated. Use your imagination. You may picture yourself simply taking their hand or smiling.

Do you need to be forgiven? If so, gently put aside any guilt or shame and ask to be forgiven. "In the name of God, I ask to be forgiven." Or you may prefer, "In the name of love, I ask for your forgiveness."

Imagine a line of light connecting your heart to theirs. This should elicit a clear response from the other person. They may want to hold you. They may smile and touch you. On the other hand, they may not want a soul connection with you right now. That's fine too. You have offered your heart. Let that gesture gather power in the higher realms.

Repeat this exercise again in several weeks if you still feel stuck with someone. And do so in a spirit of love. If it does not feel joyful to proceed, wait until it does. If you insist on trying to make a connection with someone who is not ready to connect, you deplete your energy. Wait. As long as your wish is to heal, the universe will eventually present you with the perfect opportunity to do so.

While about to embark on a business venture several years ago, I started to feel remorse for being a bully when I was a little kid. It seemed an odd connection at the time—thinking about childhood while embarking on a new business—but in retrospect the universe seemed to be pushing me to clear the old to make way for the new.

After about two weeks of feeling sullen, my phone rang. From 3,000 miles away, one of the girls I had bullied and encouraged other people to bully was on the phone. I had not spoken with this person in almost ten years. "I've been having these dreams about you and I just had to find your phone number and call," she said.

I felt stunned and relieved. I was able to apologize, from my heart, to someone I had hurt so many years earlier. Her words will always stay with me, "That's okay. I knew where you were coming from." I was forgiven with more compassion than I could have imagined.

*Everything has a ripple effect. If I touch you
with love, you will find it easier to touch someone
else with love, as they will others.*

Unfortunately, we do not always have the opportunity
to connect with someone we have wronged or with those
who have hurt us. It's not always an option to write, call or
visit. Sometimes we need closure with people who have
passed on.

Know that you can heal any unresolved pain merely
with your intent to do so. It does not have to take place on
the physical level. A thought is just as real as a phone call.

And the bonus? Every time you heal one area of discord
in your life, you give all your cells a light bath. By infusing
love into any dark place, every other aspect of your life is
brought to a higher order. That's why it doesn't work to
have one segment of your life—say your love life—in total
disarray and then expect other areas not to be affected.

Finally, the empathy exercise is important because it
affords you a preview of the life assessments you will make
after you leave the earth plane. During your life review,
which we each experience at the time of death, you see the
panoramic view. Every thought, deed or action will be
replayed for you from the perspective of every living crea-
ture that your thought, deed or action affected.

Everything has a ripple effect. If I touch you with love,
you will find it easier to touch someone else with love, as
they will others. If I give someone the finger on the high-
way, not only have I just given my own vibration a big
shot of negativity, I've also marred a moment in time for
the recipient of the gesture.

Unless the person behind the wheel is at a spiritual level where they can transmute hostile energy, my energy will cling to their aura. Now their vibration is lowered. And the life force they're sending to the world is slightly more negative than before. Because I decided to react with anger and impatience—instead of love and compassion—I put a corresponding chain of events into motion.

This is not to say people living and learning with joy are not going to feel moments of intense negative emotion. You will. These emotions, however, will become fewer and further between as you learn to live and move in the rhythm of Spirit.

In the meantime, look upon every fear-based emotion as a gift. This extraordinary present arrived to show you the situation needs more light.

At first your personality may act like a child throwing a tantrum, not wishing to cooperate. In fact, your ego will probably prefer to operate at the same level as always— attack, counterattack, retribution, withdrawal—whatever your preferred modus operandi is. Again, this is not a bad thing. Ultimately the frustration you feel at coming from "upset" over a person, place or thing will jump-start you back to your soul where there is only peace.

So if you feel a spark of anger or a flash of contempt in the course of your daily events, don't beat yourself up. Eventually you will find yourself less likely to engage others at the personality level for very long if it does not feel peaceful. Simply affirm that you will come from your higher self on every issue presented. Then seek the highest possible solution.

When you get really stymied about how to respond, take a cue from organized religion and ask, "What would

Jesus do?" or "What would Allah do?"—whatever feels right for you. Your commitment to love as a Master would love, both yourself and others, will open you up to wonderful insights and spiritual guidance.

5) Do not give your power away trying to change other people. The people who are close to you do not need to be on a spiritual path for you to continue with yours. Nor do they need to act in a specific way for you to love and honor them. Harmonizing with many different types of energy is what allows each of us to master physicality. Invariably you will come in contact with people with whom you have little in common—not just at a personality level, but also at a vibration level. Your goal? Elevate each interaction into as much love as possible...without depleting your own energy in the process.

Pursuing a path of joy means you wish joy for everyone, but you do not wish to impose joy on anyone. Dance your dance. Then relinquish the need to convert. Some people will be inspired by you, others will not.

Once you give up the need to have people around you grow, you will naturally attract souls who respect you for who and what you are. In the meantime, offer everyone compassion. But if you find yourself getting pulled into a vortex of negative energy, stop. You are not honoring yourself by continuing the interaction.

Dance your dance. Then relinquish the need to convert. Some people will be inspired by you, others will not.

It is very important to remember that you do not have an obligation to fix people's problems or wallow in the mire. In fact, if you try to present a higher solution to those not ready to solve their problems at a higher level, you set yourself up for blame.

Be judicious about where you shine your light then. Shine your light on cockroaches attending to business in a dark corner and you've got some very unhappy cockroaches. Shine your light on a kitten mewing to get out of a dark drainpipe and you've got a very happy kitten. Walk in radiance, but direct light only when it is appropriate to do so.

If you find yourself feeling drained by any situation, the universe is telling you something is out of whack. Focus on the love you can find in the experience. Then detach at the personality level.

Although focusing on what is "of God" in an interaction may seem difficult, it's important work. Otherwise expect to star in a similar drama in the future. Why? Because the universe is waiting for us to infuse every situation we encounter with love. Since all of us will one day live as our higher selves in flesh, the universe thoughtfully re-presents each difficult experience to see how "in love" we can make it.

To open our hearts on any issue is progress. Think of the avowed racist whose daughter marries a man of a different race. Accepting that marriage is a huge step back to the father's higher self. For many people, it seems the man has a long way to go. But the angels applaud gleefully. The effort it took for that particular personality to love, even a little, is far greater than most of us could imagine.

For those committed to living a life of joy, it's important to try and respond as our higher self on all issues. This means operating from the knowledge that any situation treated with less than pure love can always be reworked.

And negative impetus often serves as an important cat-alyst in this regard. If your initial feeling about say, your work environment is, "This job sucks, I never get enough time for myself. I'm always working." Good. Let the frus-tration—the lack of light—be the energy that propels you into a finer vibration.

Then list 10 reasons why you love your job. And do so with heartfelt gratitude.

"I'm grateful God presented me with this job because 1) I love the knowledge I've gained using such and such software; 2) I love the fact that I was able to conduct office meetings with poise and professionalism; 3) I love that I got to know the people in accounting…" You get the picture.

Now you are expressing sincere appreciation for experi-ences you otherwise might have overlooked in your quest to "get outta there."

Do not give your power away trying to change cowork-ers or a boss. Instead reframe in love whatever you are dealing with, and watch your new perspective construct a dynamic work environment—there or elsewhere.

Likewise, if you are dealing with a difficult family sit-uation, write down 10 reasons why you love a particular family member. This shows the universe you are com-mitted to operating from a place of honor. It does not necessarily mean all your actions will be loving—yet—but your heart is in the right place.

Love yourself. This is so important, especially when you start making significant life changes. Stay focused on who and what you are. As soon as you put your needs first, and direct your energy to doing for others only when it feels joyful to do so, your personality change is going to be noticed rather dramatically by those around you. You may find yourself cast in a negative spin cycle because you are no longer meeting other people's expectations.

For some individuals committed to the greater good, this is not a problem. For others, the universe holds up condemnation as a mirror. Are you really committed to inner peace? Are you shaky in your beliefs about love, self-respect and universal service?

Offer everyone compassion. But if you find yourself getting pulled into a vortex of negative energy, stop. You are not honoring yourself by continuing the interaction.

Most of us think not, but when disapproval rears its ugly head we immediately go into people-please mode. Accept that there will be changes at your personality level. Those who can benefit from your new integration of light will stay around. Other friends and loved ones will fall away. In reality, how different is this from everyday life? We all shed old skins and associations daily.

The difference now is that as you consciously draw more light to you, the fall-off of those who are not ready for peace will be more dramatic.

If you find your life getting turbulent as your prepare for light living, reaffirm your beliefs. Mentally state not only who you are, but who you intend to be. How do you expect to behave in the future? Write it down. And frame everything in the present tense.

"I speak only with love and compassion." "I am a warm-hearted and generous person." "I hold and radiate light." "I honor myself in all that I say and do." "Everything that is not for my higher good gently falls away."

Writing affirmations in the present tense puts the power back where it belongs—in your hands. You become less susceptible to everyone else's judgments because your Truth is there in black and white.

Not every affirmation will be accurate, yet. Writing and repeating beliefs about who you are now—and the vision you hold for yourself in the future—make it real.

Remember the words of Norman Vincent Peale in *The Power of Positive Thinking*, "If God be for me, who can be against me?" And God, Spirit or however you conceive universal Love, is there for you. You need only tap into the light around you to draw to yourself exactly what you want. "Ask and ye shall receive." "You need only the faith of a mustard seed." It's all there for us, in biblical references and experientially.

The corollary to the notion of creating the perfect life for yourself is that you need to give back. Donating money and establishing foundations is a wonderful way to serve, but you need not have these kinds of resources to be an effective light worker. There are countless opportunities where you can make a difference one on one. And the rewards you reap are far too great to enumerate here. Just ask anyone who has volunteered their time at a seniors' home or helped feed the homeless.

The world needs you and your special gifts, now. Not when everything else in your life has fallen into place. Now. And the side note is that when you take a leap of faith and let God use you to assist others, the rest of your life *will* fall into place. Giving to others leaves a void, which the universe then fills with precious life gifts for you.

Chapter VI
Children

▼

The souls coming through you are very much in tune with the transformational changes that will unfold throughout the 21st century. The kindest thing you can do for your children is to respect and recognize them for the teachers they are.

Remind your children they are glorious creatures of God with all that you say and do. What you as a parent have to offer them: advice about how to navigate the physical world. What your children offer you: lessons in love.

Your children are fresh from God. They carry with them the truth that we all come from the same Source with no essential differences between us. The outer shells we wear are tools of expression, nothing more. These old souls will try to remind you of that.

If you persist in directing your children to lower thoughts or ideas not in accordance with the world's highest vision, your children will move in different circles. This is not to say they will abandon the family necessarily, but there will be little attempt to reform or disabuse family members of lower ideas. Your children simply have too much work to do on a larger scale.

"They come through you but not from you. And though they are with you, yet they belong not to you." As Kahlil Gibran wrote so eloquently in *The Prophet*, your children are the future and you are the past. Let them soar as they intend to do with your stable, supportive backing.

Unlike what you may have experienced with your own parents, children coming into this lifetime do not need to go through the emotional experience of division and repa-ration with their parents. With each new generation, in fact, you can look forward to a deep and abiding parent/child friendship that carries on through the ages.

Your children are fresh from God. They carry with them the truth that we all come from the same Source with no essential differences between us.

This is not to say your children will not rebel. Not unlike your own generation, the preteen and teenage years tend to be systematically chaotic. Is it inevitable then that your child will at least temporarily reject your values and beliefs? No, but it is part of the blueprint that your chil-dren will separate from you in order to form close bonds with their peers.

How volatile that process is depends on their own free will. What you can do as a guide is avoid restricting their choice of clothing, friends or the kinds of music they listen to. That just makes the metamorphosis into adulthood more complicated.

For example, the tone and vibration of the music blaring from his room may be exactly what your teen needs on an energy level to get from point A to point B. Out of chaos comes order. It was true for your generation (however minor the rebellion may seem relative to today's), and it will continue to be true for subsequent generations.

The turbulence of adolescence is no different from the revolt of the toddler who refuses to use the potty. The more you fret and try to impose your will, the more the situation escalates and takes on new dimensions of antipathy. Let it be. In the end, how many 40-year-olds are still listening to Marilyn Manson and wearing the top of their pants mid-butt line? Growth at all junctures of life is inevitable. The pace of growth, and how a soul chooses to grow, is entirely self-directed. Some teens need to create more disorder and chaos than others, just as many adults did and still do.

On the other hand, it goes without saying that if you have a teen dabbling in darkness with the intent to do harm, it is a different story. Unfortunately it is not always easy to determine when and if your child has crossed the line. Most parents with school age children are with their children a scant 25 percent of the day, maybe less. You might see some antisocial behavior but what parent of a teenager does not?

Teens will be rebellious. Teens will be exposed to violence on television, Internet pornography and musical lyrics that are less than uplifting. Teens in the Western world are not unlike.

The problem is American parents also have to contend with the Second Amendment. Disaffected and troubled teens in the United States can get a loaded gun with relative ease. And that's a powerful lure. If someone isn't responding well to the pressures of adolescence—fantasizing about violence and revenge—the tools to live on in infamy are readily available.

Until the gun laws in the United States fall in line with those of Canada and the United Kingdom's, we will continue to see children killing children. As one commentator noted after the Columbine massacre, a knife doesn't kill 15 people.

Psychologists tell us the prime years for ensuring a smooth transition through adolescence occur between the ages of 8 and 12. This is the time to construct a dialogue with your child that is open, direct and respectful. After that, know that your influence will—at the very least—be shared with their friends.

And that is as it should be.

By the time a child reaches the mid to late teen years it's not going to be easy to exercise your power. Your influence—your imparting of values—preceded adolescence. Trust that the foundation you gave your children will carry them through. Don't abdicate your attempt to guide, but know that much of the growing and learning taking place during these years will be left to the judgment of your offspring. Be available to encourage and support. And set boundaries if you see something you do not like. If there is too much time spent on the Internet, move the computer into the living room.

How can you as a parent do the right thing by your children at every age?

1) First, hold the highest possible vision for your child. People tend to rise to our level of expectation for them. Teachers know that the most incorrigible students, or those who are less academically inclined, will

nevertheless rise to meet the standards of a supportive and encouraging teacher. Children are desperate to please adults even when they are busy asserting their independence. So are teenagers.

Expect the best; encourage your child; and talk about the family's long term plans. This programs the family toward soul visions. Formulate these goals through discussions about how each family member believes the unit can serve each other and the world.

Praise your child! Change the focus from what your children are doing "wrong," to everything they are doing that is wonderful.

Your influence—your imparting of values—preceded the adolescent years. Trust that the foundation you gave your children will carry them through.

2) Second, noted author and physician Deepak Chopra writes in *The Seven Spiritual Laws of Success* that it's never too early to ask your children what their special gift is— what they came to contribute to the world.

This is a far more profound way of supporting your children than insisting they achieve certain grades in school or pursue a particular career. God has no university preference. And when you leave this physical plane, Spirit is not going to add up how many A's you achieved and congratulate you accordingly.

This is not to diminish the role of a good education. On the contrary, the better the education, the more the potential for love of learning. And since learning lays the foundation for wisdom—and wisdom leads to more compassion and love for all life forms—one cannot overestimate the importance of education.

Success in school, however, or success in the workplace is not necessarily what facilitates important contribution to the world.

Some of the most undereducated people demonstrate the greatest potential to transform people's lives. The adult with Down's syndrome may inspire so much love in others that the rest of the community is gently encouraged to re-examine its priorities. A neighborhood grocery clerk may be a Master of light, so much so that your body and soul are jolted higher simply by being in his presence.

God has no university preference. And when you leave this physical plane, Spirit is not going to add up how many A's you achieved and congratulate you accordingly.

Service through love represents real world power. Men or women in the upper echelons of the corporate world or government may have power. Do you feel love in their presence?

The kind of power that has the potential to transform the world is the power of someone who radiates uncondi-tional love. It may be your gardener or garbage man, bank officer or dentist. You know it when you feel it. Whenever I'm in the presence of one of these old souls, I always feel warm and fuzzy. I usually turn to my husband and say, "I wish this person would adopt me." It is said in jest, of course, but it's an inspirational love that is so pure and kind you wish you had it around you all the time. Other people claim they feel forgiven whenever they are in the presence of such a radiant light.

3) *Be that kind of love for your children!* We all want to be. Yet many times we find ourselves falling short. When

you seem to be in danger of forgetting your own divinity, when you raise a hand to a child—even when it is with the intent to teach, not harm—you are coming from a lower vibration. Would you slap your next door neighbor if he scratched your car? Would you lovingly nurture a rose bush and then whack it because it did not bloom according to your expectations? Find a better way to teach.

When your children are misbehaving—and scaring themselves with their own loss of control—this is the time they need to see your higher self emerging. A knee jerk personality reaction does not have to be the inevitable response. Even though you may feel at wit's end, conjure all the love and respect you can muster. Let that inform the moment.

It is not easy being a parent…especially if you repeatedly tell yourself this! Proclaim that it *is* easy because you are a vessel overflowing with love for your child and all life forms. And when you feel your patience is being tested, remember: Your children will model throughout their lives whatever behavior you exhibit under pressure.

Most parents know by now that discipline is for teaching, not punishing. We also know that physical and verbal abuse leave scars that last a lifetime. Even so, the tone of voice we use with our children is often so rude we would never use it with a stranger, coworker or other family member. Listen to yourself. Turn on a tape recorder if you have to. Are you speaking to your children with a respectful tone of voice, even when your children are not responding in kind?

You are the parent. And it's important to remember that your child is a child, with corresponding childlike behavior. You may not enjoy hearing "I don't like you anymore" from your preschooler or "Stay away from me" from your teenager. Before you start labeling your child's behavior as "bad," reference a book. It is probably age appropriate.

A toddler, for example, has an exuberant curiosity. They will exercise it with or without your permission. That is what toddlers do. The more you say "no," the more you can expect to be tuned out. Baby proof your home. Then let your child do what comes naturally! It is not bad behavior when an 18-month-old bangs a pot, throws down a figurine, or refuses to share a toy. It is age appropriate.

If you don't want a precious heirloom to suffer the effects of toddler-handling, pack it away. But let your child be a child. Then when you do say no to something critical, "*No*, do not touch the hot stove," your child understands you mean business because he hasn't listened to "no, no, no" all day long.

This is not to say your home should be run by unruly youngsters. On the contrary. Children need and want boundaries. Treat your child with the same respect you would accord a friend, but remember that friendship between the two of you is what develops more significantly *after* your child has left home.

As noted author and pediatrician T. Berry Brazelton says, "Keep in mind that the longest part of your relationship with your child will be while both of you are adults. Doesn't it make sense to build a solid foundation for that friendship now?"

This means your child needs a committed compassionate guide who will help him set limits on his behavior. And it is your house, so set rules according to your priorities. Within the household parameters that you've set, however, give your children freedom. Your flexible and supportive demeanor will pay big dividends in the future.

Validation

Most parents have the best of intentions and are determined to do better than their own parents—particularly when it comes to communication. Yet while most of us encourage our children to share their feelings, we're also quick to dismiss any with which we do not agree.

The child says: "I hate Mr. Smith."

The parent responds: "I don't like it when you use the word 'hate.' Now, what happened?"

Already the parent is putting the child on the defensive by telling his son "hate" is a word he doesn't want to hear. This may be a valid concern, but this is not the time to debate semantics.

"He said I was talking. But I wasn't, it was Johnny, and he made me stand in the back of the class."

"Mr. Smith was probably just having a bad day."

This is trivial as far as the parent is concerned. End of discussion. Some parents may engage a little longer, but many of us are quick to dismiss the subject because, after all, what's the big deal? Worse, we may try to explain the teacher's point of view. Either way, the parent has effectively failed to validate the child's very real feelings of hate and humiliation in relation to the teacher.

Now imagine having a similar conversation with a good friend.

"I hate my boss."

"Oh no, what happened?"

Most of us would offer this comment or something similar—in effect, already validating the friend's feelings. After that, if you had no other support to offer other than: "Well, he was probably just having a bad day" would you expect that friend to come to you in the future? Why would she? No one—child or adult—wants to have their feelings discounted or trivialized.

Children look to adults to help them sort through, navigate and manage a formidable emotional landscape—not dismiss feelings.

Souls come into this world wise and fully formed; the emotional body is primitive by comparison. So here is your 16-year-old daughter: in control and ready to conquer the world. Yet...she is still dealing with the emotional resources of a 16-year-old. "I love him and I can't live without him" is real, is painful and cannot be seen in the context of the life experiences of a 25-year-old.

A 25-year-old knows experientially, in many cases, there will be someone else to love and adore her. The teenager's emotional development is not there yet. Telling her—however gently—there are plenty of fish in the sea does not cut it. Validate. See the hurt through the eyes of a 16-year-old who has never experienced the pain of a broken heart.

Children need the same kind of respect for their feelings we so willingly accord other adults. As a parent it's your job to teach your child that feelings are neither good nor bad, they just are. Your child has a right to feel anything he or she chooses. Do not forget that.

Bad behavior or acting out feelings in an unacceptable manner is a different story. "I know it seems the baby gets all the attention. That feels crummy. But you may not hit her, ever. What do you think we should do instead when you feel frustrated?" Then depending on the age of your child, encourage her to come up with solutions that are acceptable to both of you.

Shaming or dismissing a feeling of which you do not approve is not going to make it go away. Your higher self can shine through, though, if you can recount a time when you yourself had similar feelings.

Tell your child your story! That is immediate validation. Because now the little person sees that the most important person in her life—Mom or Dad—once felt that exact same emotion, perhaps even in a similar situation.

> *By validating instead of dismissing feelings you become*
> *a supportive player in your child's self-direction.*

Sometimes a parent resists this emotional recounting for fear it will undermine his or her authority. Just the opposite is true. When you reveal yourself, you share a part of your essence that allows your child to "see the light." Your own light becomes a guiding light—helping your children make sense of their own feelings.

By sharing and validating feelings you become a supportive player in your child's self-direction. By helping him navigate and seek solutions in the fluid world of emotion, you demonstrate what is and is not an acceptable way to behave. This builds a bond of mutual respect between parent and child that can never be replaced.

Look at the adult children who continue to go home. Now look at those adults who do anything to avoid it. As love-seeking souls we gravitate to where there is empathy, understanding and nurturing.

When parents do not validate their children's feelings, but rather disavow—"Oh, that simply isn't true"—children take an additional burden with them into adulthood. It's not just that the parent/child relationship suffers. John Gottman, Ph.D. describes it this way in his book *The Heart of Parenting*, "…The child hears the same message: 'Your assessment of this situation is wrong. Your judgment is off-base. You can't trust your own heart.' "

The end result? What Gottman calls a low emotional IQ. This leads to problems trusting one's own perception of situations, difficulty regulating emotion and self-doubt.

If you're reading this and thinking, "Hey, I can barely get a bed made, let alone commiserate with my child's every emotion," stop. Call light to you right now. Affirm that you will do what is best for your child. Invite Spirit to work with you and through you. Know that you are not alone in this endeavor to come from a more joyful, life-affirming place with your children.

Be patient with yourself. It takes practice to stop the judgment and "correction" of your child's emotions. Do it in baby steps. Start by listening to your child. Then move on to remember your own feelings of rage, fear, contempt, hate, infatuation, jealousy, jubilance…and the list goes on. Share your memories, so you are constructing common ground with this precious soul.

For the working Moms and Dads who live with the guilt they are not spending enough time with their children to validate feelings or anything else, know this: Your children came to your family for very specific reasons, including the knowledge that you would likely be working outside the home. And there is always free will. If you start to daydream about spending more time at home, make adjustments in your schedule.

If, however, you enjoy working and have career goals that comfortably coexist with a wonderful family life: terrific. You are doing more for your child than the stay-at-home parent who is harried and miserable. So release the guilt, parents. This is a different age with different values, including the ever-evolving issue of gender equity. The modeling of both Mommy and Daddy working, and both parents sharing the at-home child care, is right in line with the progressive nature of souls coming to this planet.

As love-seeking souls we gravitate to where there is empathy, understanding and nurturing.

Likewise, if you choose to stay home with your children, that is *exactly* what your family needs. The world and your children thank you for your hard work and dedication. Child rearing is a wonderful season of life. Fortify your children with all the love and support you can offer, and celebrate this very special time together. It is indeed a gift for both of you. Enjoy the time, give thanks to the universe every day and remember to make time for yourself so you are serving from a bountiful basket.

Substance Abuse

If you are one of the many parents in the world today who has lost a child to drugs or alcohol, the universe supports you. Know there is little you could have done differently.

It is easy to look back and think, "If only I'd been stricter and more vigilant...or more flexible and less demanding..." And the list goes on. Acknowledge your grief. Realize you are not alone. Nor is your child. Then be gentle with yourself. This is a choice your child has made on a very deep level—and possibly with a genetic predisposition to do so.

Start by working on a spiritual level to initiate change. Request the presence of the highest possible spiritual guides your family can attract. In some ways, spiritual intervention is even more potent than so-called traditional intervention—although each reinforces the other. Ask Spirit to surround your child with love and strength. Visualize your child healthy with a strong mind and body. Listen to the small voice within. Is there anything else you can do on the physical plane to assist your son or daughter?

Look for places in the community where you can receive support for your own pain. Once substance abuse has entered the picture, you are dealing with a soul effectively rendered unconscious. Advice and support will go largely unheeded until this child is ready to resume his or her rightful place in the world. And that time frame is entirely up to the person in question.

In the meantime, you have lost a son or daughter. And that loss needs to be grieved. Sharing with others in similar circumstances may be what you need to put issues of guilt, disappointment and anger to rest.

Growth for your loved one in this numbed state may seem improbable. But actually it is happening, even in this most unfortunate set of circumstances. Hitting rock bottom offers a unique view of the world seen only by the most courageous among us. The teaching potential afforded a former substance abuser is monumental in terms of its lasting impact on others.

The problem is often more painful for family members watching the perilous descent of those they love. Free will has brought this person to where they are now; it is their free will that will set them free.

Many addictions are overcome. Focus on and take comfort in the success stories. Again we are looking at one individual's particular growth needs. You cannot make the choice for them about how much to suffer and how much chaos to endure, but you can offer heartfelt prayer and affirmation.

Much of the success in the battle against drug and alcohol abuse comes from the light—both in this world and beyond. Support groups are a prime example of this kind of energy convergence. "When two or more are gathered in His name..." The same principle applies. When souls gather in a spirit of love, miracles unfold.

Soon we accept that we can only love,
not direct, another soul.

In the end, many people would agree the most important contribution we can make is to be a good parent. Even if we have to watch our children make choices that hurt, enrage or befuddle us, soon we accept that we can only love—not direct—another soul. Thus parenthood is a godsend, both for the growth it facilitates for ourselves and for our children.

Beyond that, however, there is something else we came to this world to do. We were not born parents. It's a role, albeit one of the most significant ones, that we have chosen for ourselves. Love your children. But save a little of yourself for the rest of the world. Decide where you want to light planet Earth and go for it.

By living a life of joy and service, you become the best possible role model for those treasured souls you love the most.

CHAPTER VII
A PEACE CALLED HOME

▼

If you wish to live in a more harmonious universe, start with the first home you've come to know: your body. If you don't feel comfortable in your own skin, you will not feel comfortable wherever that physical self takes you in this world.

Your Body

Your body works hard to function as the perfect vehicle for your soul. Its main function is to help you shine your light. If you condemn it for not living up to an idealized image your cells become infused with disappointment. The result is a polarized body and spirit.

Stop right now and give thanks for everything your body does for you. Look at the process of reproduction, digestion and circulation. Isn't it a miracle? Can you believe the intricacies of the body's design?

If there is something you'd like to change about your body, relate to your physical self with the same tenderness you would offer someone you adore. Tell your body you wish to incorporate more of a particular essence into your relationship together. Health, beauty, strength…whatever you desire, ask your body for its cooperation. Pledge that as you unleash more of these qualities at the spiritual level your body will reflect the same.

Then live as if you already have what you want.

Let's say you want to lose weight to look more attractive. Start by buying a new pair of earrings or changing your hem line. Make one small adjustment. It demonstrates concretely to the universe that your core beliefs about self are changing. If you don't know where to begin, ask yourself, "How would a person who actually feels attractive behave?"

Your body works hard to function as the perfect vehicle for your soul. Its main function is to help you shine your light.

Once you've taken the first steps, take a few more. Join an aerobics class. Get a pedicure. Practice keeping your posture straight for the whole day. You will start to see a snowball effect almost immediately. Soon all things around you will mirror your belief that you are attractive. And weight loss—when you are loving rather than condemning your body—will follow.

If you wait until you've lost the weight to allow yourself to experience the essence you want, you're doing it backwards. You're telling the universe, "One day I will be attractive, sexy, rich, fit…" or whatever, "*when I lose weight.*" The universe reflects back to you: "Yes, one day you will be." Instead isolate the soul essence you desire, and live it now.

Love, not fear, is the always operative word. If you say, "I hate the way I look, I need to lose weight now" or "My rear end is a disaster"—and then take action, you may get results but they will be results birthed in instability.

Even something as simple as thinking—uggh, look at that cellulite—and then deciding "I guess I'll go work out," is counterproductive. You've already undermined the results with the motivating factor of dissatisfaction. Proceed instead with, "Wow, what great legs I have. I'm off to the gym so I can keep looking trim and fit." It may not be true. Your thighs may have a life of their own. Your subconscious does not know this. It responds to your dominant thought—great legs—and creates that reality.

Always use love as the underlying foundation. It is the highest organizing principle of the universe. Results will be of the highest order, and thus more substantial, whenever they are birthed in light.

"I love and honor myself in every way. I treat my body well today." Cut a picture of the ideal you and put it in a top drawer. Look at it with pleasure several times a day. Trust the universe to give you exactly that or something better.

In the meantime, do not let items—such as old clothes—drag down your energy. Give them to charity. If you have "fat clothes" in your closet, give them away. If you have "thin clothes" in your closet, give those away, too. They do not reflect who you are now and you are perfect right at this moment. Treat yourself to a new outfit that reaffirms to the world what is true: You are Divine and your light is shining stronger every day.

The intelligence of your physical self gets distorted only
when underlying emotions skew the message.

If you wish to change your outer appearance or anything in your world, work backwards. 1) Isolate the
essence; 2) live as if you already have it; 3) thank your
body for giving you what you want. Genuine appreciation
and respect automatically flush each of your cells with
love. Your body will respond like a child being praised and
work even harder to please you.

Not convinced about the power of the mind to influence the body? Researchers at Manchester Metropolitan
University in Cheshire, England asked participants to
push their baby finger against a solid object, twice a week,
20 times per session. Even though participants were pushing for only five seconds each time, the first group
increased the strength of their pinkies by 33 percent. The
second group was told to simply imagine themselves doing
the exercise. Group three was told to do nothing at all.

When the results were tabulated, group three showed
no improvement. Group two, which had only *imagined*
themselves doing the exercise, had a 16 percent increase in
the strength of their baby fingers!

If thoughts alone increase muscle mass, imagine what
thought plus physical action can do for your body. Isn't it
time to start using the mind for the powerful tool that it
is—not just for body detailing—but to create whatever
you want in this world?

Consider these polygraph experiments recounted in
Deepak Chopra's book, *Ageless Body, Timeless Mind.* A
polygraph machine was attached to a subject in one
room. In another room, a different polygraph was hooked

up to a few of the man's cells, scraped from the inside of his mouth.

In a similar experiment, another man's mouth cells were hooked up to a polygraph seven miles away.

When the individuals were asked to relive a trauma, or look at stimulating pictures, the polygraphs went wild. At exactly the same time, their mouth cells in the other rooms also discharged haywire energy—recorded by those respective polygraph machines. As soon as the subjects were calm again, all polygraphs recorded a flat discharge.

Think before you think! Your cells are listening in a big way. And they are creating your physical reality based on what they hear.

What do you feed your body? Does it work for you? If it does not, relax any rigid perceptions about what makes for healthy eating. Listen to what your body wants. If you are engaged in a functional relationship with your body—you're not a compulsive under or overeater, for example—this should not present a problem. Your physical self is perfect in its knowledge about what it needs to stay nourished.

Scientists studied infants who were presented with a variety of food choices. Left to their own devices, the infants ate exactly what they needed, in just the right amount.

Two-thirds of pregnant women develop food aversions in the first trimester—when the developing fetus is at its most vulnerable. I felt terribly guilty that I could not keep down broccoli, carrots and other fruits and vegetables. I did, however, seem to do well with Southern California's famous "In and Out" burgers. Logic told me to force down the vegetables; my body gave me plenty of clues it would not accept them and led me to the burgers. So I

turned it over to divine intelligence secure in the knowledge that my body would not steer me wrong. (How could
it? I was growing a baby.)

By the second trimester I was consuming a variety of
foods, in contrast to my practically liquids-only diet of the
first trimester. My baby was born a robust nine pounds,
eight ounces.

If it works to abide by your body's very distinct pregnancy preferences and aversions, wouldn't it hold true to
listen to your body every day of your life? Your body
knows what it wants and needs. The problem is we do not
listen. We force ourselves to stay on a low fat diet, then pig
out when we're sick of the deprivation. We eagerly
embrace the latest proclamation that we need more carbo-
hydrates, only to learn the Zone diet is really where it's at.

There is no magic answer. Every single body is constructed differently.

One man profiled on the Los Angeles news several years
ago reportedly eats a Big Mac every day, and has been
doing so for the last 20 years. Is he fat? Miserable? About
to succumb to a heart attack? No. He actually looked fit,
healthy…and happy that he was listening to the intelligence of his body rather than to the latest study about
what he should not be eating.

Another woman profiled on the same news program
eats a pound of chocolate every day. Thin and happy…I
could see nothing extraordinary about this woman. She
was not an exercise fanatic nor did she seem to be obsessed
with getting a chocolate fix. She just likes to eat chocolate
daily. These kinds of eating habits may be extreme for you
or me, but apparently they are perfect for the individuals
cited here.

Assuming you are in good physical health, genuine respect for your body means trusting it when you crave guacamole and salty chips. The divine intelligence of your physical self gets distorted only when underlying emotions skew the message.

Your body is perfect—whether it is growing a baby, circulating blood or eliminating food wastes. Why would it be imperfect in knowing what it wants for fuel?

Compulsive undereating, overeating, eating out of loneliness, eating out of boredom and guilt are all symptomatic of festering emotional problems interfering with your body's communication. You need to be clear and detached from food before the "eat what you want" approach works. Once you are clear, though, you've given yourself a great gift. You can eat with joy instead of letting fear direct your food choices.

In the long run you will eat only when you're hungry and in just the right amount. And you'll be surprised at how balanced your diet really is when you eat this way, with the exception of one or two idiosyncrasies particular to each individual body.

Trust your body's message, respect the message…and continue to check the message during meditation to make sure you are receiving the input clearly. It's not like a first trimester pregnancy when the body is uncharacteristically emphatic about what it will and will not tolerate.

Listening to your body takes a little practice. Trust the process. Your body is perfect—whether it is growing a baby, circulating blood or eliminating food wastes. Why would it be imperfect in knowing what it wants for fuel?

Your job is to relax, listen and stop obscuring the message with unresolved emotional issues.

Your Home

Once you've got your body and soul working in synchronization, pledge that what you think and do in your secondary home—your house—will be of the highest vibration. It's a tall order but an important one.

Every room in your home should reflect the inner peace you feel within yourself. Dirty dishes, cluttered newspapers and old clothes piling up in closets contribute to a breakdown in the flow of energy. Keep it streamlined.

Ideally your household objects should also radiate peace. Inanimate objects absorb and retain energy, so watch what kind of life force circulates in your home.

Arguments and acts of violence make a distinct impression on objects—more so than a simple negative comment—because they are infused with intense emotion. So if you're tempted to break a dish, hit the wall or throw a shoe to really make a point during an argument, think again. That's probably not the kind of energy you want lingering in your house after the argument is over. And it will linger: in your furniture, walls, carpet and everywhere else in the radius of the outburst.

The best way to keep your house clear is to take disagreements outside. Say your piece on the porch. If you live in a high rise, step onto the balcony. The beauty of this is that it tends to put a quick check on gratuitous yelling because after all, "what would the neighbors think?" And besides, who wants to debate in inclement weather?

Plunging temperatures and freezing rain have a way of curtailing the most heated discussions.

On the other hand, if the weather's good take a walk with the person who upset you. Allow yourself to vent through exercise and outdoor dialogue. The benefits are numerous. Nature heals. Trees, plants and flowers are adept at absorbing negative energy. And by exercising while you release your anger—or even shortly thereafter—your aura stays relatively free of any weighty debris that would otherwise accumulate.

If you're tempted to break a dish, hit the wall or throw a shoe to really make a point during an argument, think again. That's probably not the kind of energy you want lingering in your house.

Finally, your home truly stays a sanctuary. The only thoughts that gather there are love-based. And your objects absorb and reflect this love back to you.

Along the same line, it's important to be judicious about bringing used furniture into your home. Since you are inviting other people's energy to sit in your house, do so only after careful consideration.

Used baby items are a welcome provision for many new parents. At an energy level they also tend to enhance rather than deplete light. The pure love exchanges that go on between parent and child function at an exceptionally high level the first few years, in almost every family. So unless you know of specific events that may have over-shadowed this exchange, used baby items can be a nice addition to your own family's energy.

Other used furniture—including couches, tables and beds—should be added to your home only after you have checked first with your inner self. Tune into the piece, then honor whatever feelings arise.

After moving cross-country our family was in the market for a used couch. I stumbled across what sounded like a beautiful, comfortable couch at a reasonable price. The owner sounded lovely on the phone, but spent much of the time enumerating her illnesses. She wanted to sell the sofa because she was due to have surgery and needed something sturdier to sit in. Her husband had also just died.

The logical part of me said, "This is a deal, let's go for it." My higher self instructed me to move on. It's not that the couch was bad. On the contrary, my impression of the sofa was that it resonated strength and service. But energy accumulation of illness and sorrow needs to be counter-balanced authoritatively from the outset. I wasn't up for it. My own energy was already scattered from the move. I decided to pass.

If you find it dubious that objects—couches or otherwise—actually gather and amplify energy, touch a treasured piece of china. Can you discern a mood or subtle fragrance not coming from you? That's the energy of the object. And it's an accumulation of the predominant feeling of every person who has held, touched or been near it.

Every loving emotion resides in your home. Every negative emotion also takes root. The good news is that negative thoughts dissolve in the light of one act of love. So if you've let too many arguments arise in your home—or engaged in too many thoughts of fear and sorrow—commit that from now on you will only love within your dwelling.

Never push away feelings of a lower vibration in an attempt to keep your home "clear." Anger, frustration, jealousy and fear are all emotional gifts you give yourself to heal. If, however, you catch yourself ruminating—when you can't restore inner peace—the optimal path is one that takes you outdoors.

When you allow yourself to walk in God's world with a sense of wonder at the grace of a power far greater than your problems, you invite calm to your being. And your feelings have a supportive space in which to heal.

Your Neighborhood

When Hillary Clinton wrote *It Takes a Village* critics lambasted the notion. Political opponents suggested the very title encouraged parents to abdicate the moral responsibility of raising a child.

Anyone who actually read the book understood its purpose: to remind us of the joys and benefits of neighborhoods and community. This translates to care—not just for one's own family—but for other people's children and families, too.

As we make inroads into the 21st century, the trend of upgrading to larger homes and isolated communities is already subsiding. Many families, stung by a hectic pace, regret they scarcely recognize their neighbors across the street much less know their names.

Especially for the benefit of one's own children, who may not be fortunate enough to be surrounded by extended family, many parents are abandoning life in the suburbs. Cohousing, or community-based living, is becoming an attractive alternative.

Cohousing does not function with a common ideology. Nor is there a sharing of money. Rather these communities are constructed for the sole (and soul) purpose of fostering a sense of goodwill among neighbors. Simple things are shared by those who wish to partake: child care, community dinners and neighborhood entertainment.

Privacy—and indeed each house is relatively secluded from the others—is still paramount for most families living in these kinds of communities across the United States. If and when families want to join others in laughter and celebration, group interaction is easily accessible.

It's also true that while an increasing number of souls are ready for this kind of integrated community living, most are not. There is an inherent suspicion that this kind of village interaction is intrusive or worse: The group exists to further some kind of religious or political agenda.

In fact, most families living in a cohousing community have different religious backgrounds and engage in dissimilar recreational hobbies. They also hold jobs ranging from doctors and lawyers, to homemakers and musicians. Lifestyles run the gamut. What is similar is the energy vibration, which in turn creates the pull to come together as a group.

From a spiritual perspective, two heads are better than one. When people congregate to effect positive change—by creating a loving community, for example—the energy available to that group is greater than say, the energy available to a single family. Blessings multiply as more likeminded souls gather in a spirit of cooperation.

Children feel a part of a wider community and rejoice in the company of other adults who have care and concern for them. Parents feel the love and support of other families in the neighborhood. No one relinquishes autonomy, but there is more of a commitment to helping and interacting with others.

This contrasts with neighborhoods of today where there may be a common thread in terms of socioeconomic status, but the spiritual vibrations may run from one extreme to the other. Disputes with neighbors over property lines or other trivial issues occur as dissimilar energies clash. Even more common: The simple indifference people feel towards one another in the neighborhood. They're literally not on the same wavelength.

> *Blessings multiply as likeminded souls gather*
> *in a spirit of cooperation.*

The quest for joyful living will pull people to seek love within their community circle. The dynamics of each neighborhood will peak as people are naturally drawn to communities that resonate similar energies to their own.

The lack of a common ideology in co-op communities makes the living easy. Since there is no religious fervor or political dogma, people are not bound by anything other than to pursue their own joy (whatever that may be) and enjoy the community as a support system.

And support system means different things to different people. Some will be drawn by the concept of having other trustworthy adults available to interact with their children. Others will simply enjoy a peaceful environment with other likeminded souls. Still others may spend much of their time alone secure in the knowledge that if they want friendly interaction or a homecooked community meal, it's available.

Diversity of inhabitants will be the norm. Different age groups, different races, different family units will come together in a spirit of cooperation. People who judge others on the basis of outward appearances might discover a good amount of spiritual growth is necessary before this type of environment would feel right for them.

Co-op communities have been common in Scandinavia since 1980. Those sprouting across the United States are still a work in progress. There is currently a waiting list to buy homes in many of them, with some applicants being selected by lottery.

Not to be outdone, even traditional home builders across the United States are designing with an eye to old-style interactive neighborhoods. Porches, sidewalks, smaller streets with parking strictly behind the houses…all of these design elements facilitate interaction with neighbors and will eventually become mainstream.

Whether a co-op community or an old-style neighborhood, these are the trends that will inspire as we move through this century. The isolation of modern day living will push more seekers of peace to pursue the concept of growth through joy—not just in their personal lives—but in their neighborhoods, too.

Chapter VIII
Joy Above, Joy Below

▼

Whatever you conceive in your mind can be brought into the physical realm—as long as you are prepared to release your expectations about how and when it must be achieved. If you think it, so too can you live it.

Most of you know there is more to life than what you are living right now. Yet your thoughts are scattered when it comes to achieving what you came here to do. It's like looking through a dirty window pane: You can see only a glimpse of what awaits you.

As you start to live your life with integrity—according to your values and truth—the window pane clears. Suddenly what is possible reveals itself in all its glory. And the universe rejoices for the clarity you have attained.

Are you ready and clear at every level to create heaven on earth? If the following information feels like truth for you—the answer is yes.

- Repeated patterns are the universe showing you you're stuck. Every unpleasant situation will recur in different forms until darkness is replaced with love. This you know.

- In truth and with integrity is how you approach your life. You extend your hand in light. Sometimes that love will be reciprocated at a higher level, sometimes not. People may not be ready to do the work to release the struggle. You never allow your own energy to be compromised; instead you comfortably hold your love from a distance.

- Compassion serves as a hallmark of your existence. Everyone has their story. Everyone needs their pain validated before it can be processed and released. You listen to your loved ones, your children, the disadvantaged...and give your time to those who want to be heard.

- You ask to do God's work to heal those individuals who desire joy and abundance, but are caught in a cycle of fear and pain. You never preach...because you know everyone is exactly where they prefer to be right now. Yet you allow your own joy to be contagious to those who want a different way to live and learn.

If this is how you are living your life, praise God. You are serving the world as an instrument of the Divine. This does not mean you are now officially exempt from lower self directives: "I don't want to do this or that, so I'll just throw a tempter tantrum right now and get my way." Nor does it mean you will float like an angel through the world, hugging everyone you meet and spreading glad tidings. This is not what it means to be living in the higher flow and growing through joy.

What it does mean is that your personal moments of turmoil will become fewer and further between. And when erratic emotions do occur, you will be able to calm yourself—and seek a higher solution without thrashing about indefinitely in fear and confusion.

Likewise, you will move through the world in peace. And you will find your greatest treasures lie within yourself.

You are not impacting this world alone. If you are a person who seeks to unify rather than divide, if you ask yourself, "what can I contribute?" rather than "what can I get?", how can you not stand with God? God is in all of us, but each of us can act in un-Godly ways and God steps aside.

When we act in ways that are of God—peace, love and compassion—all that is light and glorious illuminates our path. The world of Spirit is available to each of us in direct proportion to the amount of guidance we are open to receive. Other world servers join us, certainly on the spiritual plane, but many will also start to appear in our place of business or in our neighborhood. You are never alone once you intend to serve from the deepest part of your soul. Together with others you will be able to move joy above, into manifested joy below.

> *You are never alone once you intend to serve*
> *from the deepest part of your soul. Together with*
> *others you will be able to move joy above,*
> *into manifested joy below.*

Do not go about your day to day existence in fear then. Fear can be your friend when it provides the impetus to clean the dirty window. It is not your friend when it is the only hand you hold as you walk through your day. Shift your focus away from fear and its offspring by focusing on the greatest power available: Love.

Author and lecturer Marianne Williamson reminds us that even when we are sick with worry over finances, our health, our job...*we can still give love*. We can find love and give love in every moment! Fear can't help but shrink in the face of such a formidable power. If you offer love to anyone or anything who needs you—even when your heart is breaking—the distortion of fear fades away. And the rest of your problems are put into a proper perspective.

Our ego or lower self is a great instructor because it reminds us of what is not true. The mind plays many games. It thinks it is helping by scaring us with "what ifs."

A fearful voice is a voice with many layers. Some of our lower self voices hold the anger of parents; others echo the sentiments of people who hurt us in the past. In all cases the fearful voice takes the misguided approach of protecting us by frightening us. Listen carefully, recognize the distortion, then calm the fear by loving it as you would a scared puppy.

The voice of the higher self or soul is never fearful, angry or condemning. It is the wisest part of you—reminding you with soothing words and gentle direction that you are a gift to this world. If you allow it, your soul can and will direct your life. When fears arise from your personality the higher self will gently transform these doubts by embracing them with love.

If, however, you deny your true self and let your ego move you through the world, you will continue to create crises over and over again. Not until you get back to the part of you that is real will you truly live in peace.

Thus there is really very little mystery here. Our physical body is the vehicle we have chosen to experience the world of lower self. In the process of living what we are not, we remember Truth. As we remember Truth, we light the illusion. We bring our mental, physical and emotional instruments under the direction of our spirit. The worlds of higher and lower self merge—and the universe beholds the music of our soul.

"You can't make a silk purse out of a sow's ear." No matter how much you work on making the personality more pleasant or less ego-driven, it will not satisfy your quest for "perfection" if the mind still directs the course of your existence.

The mind will never be the glory that is you! It is an instrument only, just as your body is an instrument of expression by which you can do the bidding of the intellect (war and competition) or of the heart (peace and cooperation).

Integrate it. Ask that your higher self and lower self unify so that all aspects of you in this life function as a manifestation of Spirit. This is the only way to take away the pain. This is the only way to live as a joyful being in every moment. "As above, so below" becomes possible when you are willing to concede that doing it on your own has not worked. And handing it over to paternalistic version of God has not worked either.

Do not expect the universe to do it for you while you sit back and wait for a miracle to happen. True transformation occurs when you take God's hand and declare, "Hey Spirit, this isn't working. I'd like to know peace and joy and abundance but it ain't happening. Show me a better way."

The way that will be shown—when you approach God in a spirit of cooperation—will be presented lovingly and with support. Nothing will be given to you before you are ready at every level to receive it.

The worlds of higher and lower self merge, and the universe beholds the music of our soul.

If you still have abundance issues, or beliefs about money that are distorted, you will be asked to do the work to bring those unhealed areas into a higher vibration. Likewise, if you have forgotten to celebrate yourself, you will not be presented with a loving relationship until you have remembered who you are.

There is no quick fix here. But there is relief. When you have surrendered the need to control you may still flounder temporarily in the darkness, but the shift is now palpable. Your awareness of what's real and what's illusion is coming into focus. The window pane is clearing.

Exercise One
Bring it Back

Physical manifestation is slow on the earth plane. This we know. Because of the lag time between dreams as thoughts, and dreams as physical reality, it is important to mobilize *all* your energy from the outset. And you may find that energy lingering in some unexpected places.

Anywhere on this earth where you experienced a strong emotional response portends loss of soul light.

If you had a childhood home fraught with difficulties, you need to call back energy left there. If you experienced a love affair that hurt your heart, you need to call back energy relinquished to that relationship. Anywhere there was severe hurt or pain indicates a probable loss of your energy.

Get quiet and ask Spirit to lead you through this exercise. Mentally request the return of all soul light lingering in or around houses, neighborhoods, countries, people, places or things you've encountered in your life. Name that energy as your own; ask that it return to you in a spirit of love.

See your light return like falling stars against a dark sky backdrop. Picture yourself with arms held wide embracing this life force as it merges with the rest of your energy.

After you've performed this exercise the first time, take cues from your inner self about how often to repeat it. Once a month over a six month period is usually ideal. Your body needs to process the returned light so be careful not to rush the process.

Exercise Two
Keep it Clean

Living and moving in the higher flow does not mean your aura—the human energy field—is impervious to negative energy. If your emotional body is calm and centered, the life force around your body reflects peace. When your emotional self is in turmoil, your energy mirrors unrest.

If you find yourself falling into despair—and this will happen less frequently as you learn to live in the higher flow—quickly ask Spirit what the situation is showing you. How can you add light and lift the experience into love? Once you feel even a slight shift in consciousness (usually after a few days of introspection), turn your attention back to your energy body for "grooming."

In her book *Light Emerging* author and physicist Barbara Brennan offers this slightly modified technique to clean your aura. Be sure to do the inner work first. Otherwise, if you perform this exercise before your emotions are at peace, you will simply recreate a discordant energy.

Using one pound of sea or Epsom salts, and one pound of baking soda, add the combination to a very warm—not hot—bath. Relax in the bath, on your back, for about 10 minutes. Dunk your head briefly under water so the energy field around your head and neck is also included. Lift your head up, turn over and spend another ten minutes on your tummy.

After the bath apply sunscreen and follow with ten to 20 minutes in the sun. If you can go outside, good; if not, lie down in a sunlit room. Follow with a shower.

You may feel tired and heavy after this exercise. Do not be alarmed. That is part of the process. Nap if you can. The sluggishness will be disappear after an hour or so, and you will feel completely revitalized.

Although this exercise lends itself to a once a month treatment your regular shower can also incorporate similar aura cleansing properties. Simply affirm that the shower water clears away any grime that may have attached to your light body.

Have you ever noticed some of your best ideas come to you in the shower? If so, you're probably unconsciously cleaning more than just your physical body. Close your eyes. As the shower water pours over you pretend it is a mist of whatever color your energy field needs. Absorb that mist and breathe deeply. When it feels like a struggle to continue, stop.

If any of these exercises seem a little out there, that's okay. You may need to suspend your disbelief occasionally. The left brain, rational side of your personality sometimes needs to take a back seat to the unseen world. Respect any feelings of trepidation that may arise. An exercise ill-suited to you at this time may be just what the doctor ordered five years from now.

Be patient with yourself. Where you are right now, and exactly how much spirituality you want to incorporate into your everyday life, is perfect for you.

Where you are at this moment, and exactly how much spirituality you want to incorporate into your everyday life, is perfect for you.

On the other hand, if your reluctance to get up and glow is a question of indifference—or laziness—let go of the need to control just for a moment. Allow the light of your soul to guide you.

Your soul waits patiently for you. It always bides its time until you are ready to respond to its gentle broadcasts and encouragement.

Exercise Three
Light the Dream

Part I

Harness the light of the world, then—as soon as you are ready to build the life of your dreams. And do so with a sense of fun and playfulness.

Start with basic meditation, keeping in mind there is no "correct" way to meditate. You can meditate walking through the woods, watching the sunset or staring at a roaring fire. Meditation is about a feeling of reverence for our world—and becoming more centered within yourself so that you are one with it.

If, however, you've never allowed yourself to fall into the sense of timelessness that comes through deep meditation, here are a few tips.

Lie on your stomach. Breathe in deeply. Feel your abdomen expand, starting with the lower section, then moving up to and including the upper chest. The nice thing about this position is that you will feel your entire torso press against the ground. Enjoy it. That pressure will keep you focused on your breathing, ensuring it stays rhythmic and deep.

After five minutes or so, sit up and assume the lotus position. Or you may prefer the child's pose, which is very much like the prayerful position Muslims assume. Listen to your body. Allow it to move effortlessly into the most relaxing position for you.

Now sit quietly. Affirm that whatever information you need to know comes to you—from your highest possible spiritual connection.

Part II

If you have allocated 15 minutes a day to meditation, devote roughly the first half of the session to breathing work and opening to receive. Use the second half to work actively with the light.

When you are peaceful and relaxed from meditation, open your arms. This allows full physical expansion of your heart center—the area between your breastbone and collar bone. Picture that heart center glowing like a ball. Now drop your arms. Allow your body to be lifted up and out in your imagination.

Come to rest at the edge of a beautiful pool. This pool of water may sparkle in an old country garden or shimmer at the base of a mountain range. It does not matter where you find it. The key is this water represents power—both the power of the universe to give you the life of your dreams, and the power of you to create it.

Stand in the water. Using your feet as a magnet, slowly pull the energy of the pool up through your body.

Keep this life force circulating quickly—up and out through the crown of your head. You are now radiating layers and layers of golden light. If someone were to see you, your physical body would be barely discernible because you are pulsating light ad infinitum.

Plug into one of your dreams now, the highest vision you hold for yourself.

If it's a new house, see that home before you. Feel the joy associated with your vision. Connect your heart center to the home and paint details with your light: rose bushes in the backyard, a sunken garden tub...whatever feels magnificent for you. If you want your neighborhood to radiate a terrific childlike energy, surround your home with a color that represents vibrancy for you. If you'd prefer a more peaceful cooperative energy, surround your house with blue or green mist.

The more detail you use, and the more you evoke a feeling of awe as you mentally paint your image, the more power ascribed to your light work.

> *You can create anything you want, but you may not impose your will upon another. Visualizing Michael Jordan bringing you breakfast in bed is probably not going to manifest.*

Keep in mind that you can create anything you want, but you may not impose your will upon another. Visualizing Michael Jordan bringing you breakfast in bed is probably not going to manifest. It's okay to visualize Michael there anyway or whomever you wish. Just be flexible in terms of who you actually get! Focus on the qualities represented; then allow the universe to give you someone who evokes similar feelings of passion, admiration or love.

Light is a wonderful tool to use for all kinds of manifesting exercises. A house is just one example. Use the same principles to create the perfect job, a car or any other scene you wish to see played out in your life: winning an award, receiving a degree or sailing around the world.

Before you end your magnetizing session, identify the soul essence of what each achievement means to you. In the case of a new home your house may represent peace, freedom or security. Whichever soul quality feels the strongest for you, wrap your dream in a bubble of that essence. Allow it to float out in the universe and gather the energy of other likeminded wishes. Wait, without despair, until that vision bursts into your physical world.

Keep in mind that working with the light may leave you a little tired, a little warm or a little cold. Your body is not used to being such an active participant in the higher realms. Do not push yourself. Try to get more sleep than usual when magnetizing.

If you get weepy and somewhat emotional after working with the light, that's normal too. One gentleman went home and watched the movie "Rudy" after a day of lightwork. He spent most of his viewing time in tears. Yes, it is a sad movie but...

The bottom line is your emotional responses may be a little exaggerated. Likewise the extra addition of light to your home may impact all members of your household, including family pets. After one light-intensive seminar our family's furry friends slept for days. It was just a little too much energy for everyone to easily process.

Do not rush it then. Proceed slowly—until your physical body gets used to actively cocreating the highest possible visions you hold for yourself and the world.

Exercise Four
Service from Your Soul

As you learn to live more fully as your soul in physical form your relationships with other people will naturally deepen. In every moment, with every encounter, you will eventually ask: What can I offer this person? How may I serve you? It becomes a shift from lower self interaction to higher self interaction.

Most of us don't consciously mingle with people and think, "Hmm, what can I get from this person?" But we do reach out to get something. Usually it's for the intangibles: respect, desire, approval or admiration.

Ultimately we learn to give ourselves everything we need in every moment. Then our interaction with others becomes more easily service-based. "How may I assist you?" becomes the unspoken dialogue that in turn awakens another to their own power.

As you move through your day, serve. When you are at the grocery store, in the bank or walking your dog—smile from your soul. Playfully send a mental love burst to a baby or to someone who's grumpy and having a bad day.

When you interact with a coworker, shift the mental rapport to the spiritual just for a moment. Silently ask: What can I offer you in this working relationship?

Most of us don't consciously mingle with people and think, "Hmm, what can I get from this person?" But we do reach out to get something.

As you meditate, devote part of your time to serving the world. The more people who hold a vision in light—finding a cure for cancer, for example—the faster it will be happen. People tend to feel powerless, and so overwhelmed by all the problems in the world, we do nothing except think, "Thank God it's not me."

Make a commitment. Decide that every day at the end of your meditation you will picture yourself jumping up and down as you read a newspaper headline declaring: Cure for AIDS. Hold that vision. Imagine everyone around the world rejoicing as they read the same headline.

The next day in your meditation see the headline proclaiming: Heart Disease Eradicated. You get the idea. You won't run out of illnesses. There are enough man-created diseases—designed to get each of us back to Spirit—to keep the world busy in meditation for quite awhile.

Don't just shrug your shoulders and shudder, "Oh, it's terrible." Be proactive. You do not need money to make a difference. You do not need your life to be working perfectly to make a difference. All you need is the understanding that when one of us suffers, it is you and it is me. It is all of us. Affirm that a cure for every disease has been found, and that no one need suffer again to remember we are God.

CHAPTER IX
PARTY WITH GOD

▼

To exist in a state of pure love is to exist in a state of divinity. Rather than moments punctuated by fear, a person who chooses to grow from joy lives in moments punctuated by transcendent love.

Pure or transcendent love is the highest form of love: love that is one with God. When one passes into pure love, time stands still. Not only is there a sense of losing one's self in the moment, there is a feeling of connection—of being Home.

When you first commit to live in joy these moments of bliss may be few and far between. Then as you begin to attract all things of a higher order in your life, you will draw more of these "warm and fuzzy" moments to you—when everything seems right with the world.

If you are at a loss as to what these moments consist of, remember when you felt a deep spiritual connection with another soul. There will not be a memory of pain or longing here. That is a relationship of a different sort. Rather this bliss is characterized by a feeling—however brief—that transcends time. It is mysterious in some way. To remember is to consciously draw more of the same to you. So allow yourself to focus on those instances in your life when you felt safe and centered and loved.

I remember cuddling in the arms of my granddaddy, a big gentle soul who radiated love and light. The memory is one of warmth, peace and security. You may liken it to a cocoon, for that is what it really is. When there is a love exchange at such a high order, souls merge their auras to create a cocoon of light.

Shortly after one of the first dates I had with my husband, we walked outside onto the beach. It was dark and chilly, and we were in our sweatshirts and bare feet. As we hugged under the stars, just for a moment time stood still. I was Home. This sense of merging with another soul in a warm protective sphere of light doesn't happen very often. When it does, you will not forget it. It is different from a hug of passion, a hug of comfort or even a hug of joy.

Babies free float with their parents in a protective cocoon of light from the very beginning. Coming from the light they remember little else. Only now they have a body. What at first seems so foreign is eventually mastered. And soon the baby learns to recreate the pleasures of light in physical form. It's easy, too, because infants have such willing partners in the pure love exchange: mommy and daddy.

This first experience of bliss in the physical body is what we as adults will seek to recapture throughout our lives. And it may take some effort. Rather than effortlessly exchange love with another soul, a natural caution prevails. This is true for each of us for the same reason: Once a baby understands it is separate from its parents there is a "disconnect." The association of love—with longing and separation—begins.

Since the physical planet is a place to experience complexities of energy, the process quite naturally begins the day we enter our body. Yet regardless of our first love imprint—or subsequent sources of love—we remain love-seeking missiles. We eagerly forge on to create and experience love in many ways and shapes throughout our lives.

When one passes into pure love, time stands still. Not only is there a sense of losing one's self in the moment, there is a feeling of connection—of being Home.

To recapture a memory of pure love in your own life, start by remembering a meaningful bear hug. Most hugs are perfunctory in nature. There is little, if any, connection to Spirit. But you may have experienced a few in your lifetime that were different. Call them to memory. That hug says, "I love you, heart to heart." If you felt embraced by light and were momentarily suspended in time, you experienced an encounter of divine love.

The moments you recall are likely to have been brief but profound nonetheless. Until recently, our bodies were not structured to retain a significant amount of light. The exchange had to be short. Luckily that is changing. As we relinquish the notion that life needs to be a struggle, we are building a stronger foundation of love around us. We hold more light—and radiate an energy from which all may draw strength.

If I walk into a room committed to spread love—regardless of what may have come before—there is light there. The room will be impacted by my presence as I radiate energy and lift the room's vibration. Depending on the receptivity of the other people, that light will either multiply or remain static. No one is forced to join in light and celebration. And indeed, some souls may be better served by remaining in relative darkness.

Likewise I may enter a room filled with personal fear and negativity. My energy may be dark with disappointment and regret. This, too, impacts a room. Others there may find my gray mood complements their own feelings of discontent. Light, however, is always available for the asking. And if there are other people in the room radiating light, and I am the least bit receptive, I will plug into—and lift—my own energy with ease.

As the world awakens to the power of joy as a means for navigating life, expect to see more dramatic examples of pure love in your own life. Every time we choose joy over struggle we light ourselves and the world. The catch is that your energy body shines in direct proportion to how much personal clearing you've done. You can't radiate peace if your energy holds fear. You cannot glow if you have not healed.

What needs to be healed in you? Anything, past or present, that does not resonate with love. If you think of something in your life, and it conjures any feeling other than love, it is not functioning at its most harmonious vibration. Spirit will encourage you to move it into a finer frequency—so that all your experiences play in the joyful range.

Ask for God's help in finding the highest possible solution to any problem that plagues you. You do not have to do a major life overhaul, but you do need to take responsibility for getting your life in order. This means being resourceful and creative with every problem that presents itself.

The darkness within you—whatever is not lit by love—is never to be never disparaged or rejected. As quoted by Pat Rogest in *Emmanuel's Book*, "Your less evolved areas have a right to be. They whisper of things past. They whisper of confusion…Look to understand your negative feelings as a loving mother would understand a confused and frightened child."

There is, however, no need to linger in your dark places. View them as a compassionate yet disinterested third party would. Then ask, "Where has the fear, the separation from God, obscured the love in this situation?"

You don't have to listen to your inner messages, of course. You make the choice about how much fear to embrace. And depending on the toxicity of the emotions, your body may say "enough is enough" before you do— with the end result being physical illness. Spirit, however, will give you plenty of gentle prodding before a breakdown of the old occurs. Simply be still and listen. Make small changes daily with the intent to manifest as the radiant being of light you are.

As we relinquish the notion that life needs to be a struggle, we are building a stronger foundation of love around us. We hold more light and radiate an energy from which all may draw strength.

Love well every single day. Form groups. Call together friends, family and neighbors to your home in celebration. Encourage others in the group to reciprocate so there are separate celebrations of light in each home. This way there is a sharing of festivities; one home doesn't become the "church," creating a leader or minister. Not to say others may not inspire you—inspiration is terrific. Just remember where the highest power of God resides. In you.

Power exists in numbers. And there is divinity in ceremonies. Weddings are a prime example. When two souls unite in marriage, their union is bathed with the love, hopes and expectations of the people attending. A wedding becomes a wonderful opportunity to infuse sacred energy into an already special commitment. Not only are guests arriving in a spirit of joy and celebration, but the universe awaits with anticipation to see what light this couple will add to the world.

A wedding or any kind of ceremony proclaiming love, translates into a big-time love infusion—both from the invited guests and from the heavens. This the couple carries with them as they move forward into the future, regardless of whether their union is meant to be brief or long term. It is wholeheartedly special either way and that is affirmed on their wedding day.

Don't wait until somebody's marriage to party with God! Create a gathering of light beings and celebrate in love, once a week or once a month. Revel in the glory of fellowship. You need not share common lifestyles, although chances are you will attract others of a similar vibration.

The intent of your group may vary, too. It may start as a healing unit—perhaps for its own members. Later it may evolve into a beacon of light—shining collective energy on world problems or geographical areas needing hope and transformation.

Whatever purpose you wish your group to serve, keep it light and in light. Celebrate as though it were a wedding! Dress up. Laugh. Serve delicious food and drink. Light candles, join hands, give meaningful bear hugs. Invite the angels to direct your group. And acknowledge the presence of other spiritual guides who merge their energy with yours to effect change in the world.

If you allow it, your group can function as a divine instrument. Write a mission statement, so the group's energy stays focused. Once the light you have directed has served its purpose, it will feel heavy to continue. Reverse course. Something else in the universe needs your attention.

The work you do as a group will be sweet and soothing. As light workers you will have the power to illuminate any area of darkness on which you choose to focus. Yes, you may do this individually through your thoughts and prayers. Since there is a tremendous force in collective energy, make the most of it. Rejoice in the power that you as an individual, and as part of a loving group, have to heal the world.

I once had a dream where souls were dancing with the Divine. I was hanging around a post by the stage, sort of my usual place in life. Suddenly God wanted to dance with me. Me? Come on. "As if"…but in my dream it was okay. I was okay. I was more than okay. I was great. And so are you. And so are we all. God wants you to dance with joy, every day. It is not a dance reserved for the select few.

Commit to touch everything you encounter then with your unique capacity to love.

The busy mind is easily distracted by things of little importance. That's part of the challenge of living in a body and functioning in a physical world. It's easy to view the mind as the instrument of life, the means for navigation, the determinant of success. That is the illusion.

The mind is inconsequential if it is not doing the bidding of the heart. All the success in the world is irrelevant if the heart is not happy. We know this to be true, yet somehow we put our faith in the belief that if only we had one thing in particular—a new car, a better job, a more substantial cash flow—our hearts would be glad.

If we let a loving heart guide us, the illusions that take us away from our immutable perfection fade. Every day and every moment will be a party with Spirit because love is the highest of all vibrations. That means loving the self first and honoring all that is glorious about our essence. Then when we are filled with the love and wonder of self, we move on to touch others in compassionate ways.

To lay the foundation for a life of joy, give yourself the gift of things you love and get rid of the things you don't. It sounds so simple. Yet how many of us remain chained to people, places and things that no longer serve us?

If you are beholden to any situation out of a sense of obligation you are dishonoring yourself. If you are bound to a situation that claims to be of love, but actually causes you pain, you are sabotaging your inner peace. Shift relationships to a higher level. If the other people involved wish to join you at that level, glorious. If not, release them gently and allow them to do as they wish without your participation.

Many of us have a strong connection with creatures of the furry variety. Our animal friends give us such deep, abiding, unconditional love that it's hard not to be spiritually elevated when surrounded by such splendid energy.

Every time you speak with another person
send them love through your eyes.

Invite animals to come in and share your home. The love exchange with these companions is as real and powerful as any love you will experience. If I feel my mind is distracted from the Truth of my existence I connect with my animals. Hold, cuddle, baby talk…you have not only lowered your blood pressure says the medical establishment, you've also added a few years onto your life. Perhaps more importantly, each time you offer a loving touch and kind words to an animal you are in service to another soul.

Don't forget to fill your house with flowers and plants to reflect nature's beauty. Even individual rocks have a special energy; invite a rock into your home if it feels right. Whatever gives you the ability to relax and remember what's real, versus what's superfluous, is what should surround you.

Every time you speak with another person send them love through your eyes. This is easy with people you actually love. You'll know you have it mastered when you can do it with people with whom you have little connection. You raise your own energy every time you look past someone else's fear and anger, and offer love instead.

Make a difference with your touch. When you are moved to touch someone or something, do it with all the love of your soul. Be sure to listen to your intuition, though, before you move into someone else's space. We've all had the experience of hugging someone who stood as rigid as cardboard.

It's not a bad thing you wanted to communicate compassion at a given moment. Nor is it a bad thing that person was not open to receive. But to avoid an energy drain on your end, do not put out loving energy where it's not wanted. Eventually Spirit will have you moving in circles where your touch and words are needed, at almost every juncture.

Many souls are awakening to their divinity. These are the beings who need your guidance and inspiration. Wait for the time when you are in a place to give, and receive, love. In other words, please do not spin your wheels giving to those who do not wish to receive.

Spot love. Pick someone out of a crowd and connect their heart to yours through an imaginary stream of light. Think the words, "God bless you" or a simple, "I love you." And why shouldn't you love them? You are already connected with every life form in this universe. *We are all one.* Rejoice in that connection. The person with whom you connect, just for that one second in time, will absolutely feel it. Allow that soul to use your love however they choose.

Create a big dream for yourself. Decide on your legacy here and now. And snap to it. The world needs your gifts. I get a big kick in the pants every time I find a gray hair. I get an immediate rush of knowledge that I'm going back to the Light. Holy moly. I'm just going about my day-to-day business, but then it hits me: "I'm on the way out." Gray hair is not a good sign. To me it signifies my time is finite in a big way and I'd better do what I came to do, now.

Ask yourself where you can spread the most love. You're not spreading love if you're motivated solely by making money, being famous or owning the nicest car on the block. And the deepest part of your self knows this. These circumstances can absolutely coexist with service to others. Pursued for their own sake, however, they hold little weight. If something is born of self-interest only, it does not have the same momentum as something born from a desire to serve.

> *It's easy to view the mind as the instrument of life, the means for navigation, the determinant of success. That is the illusion.*

Only you can know where your part in the world lies. But if you listen to the small voice within God will remind you. *Listen.* And do not abdicate the responsibility to follow through on what you hear. Small steps are all you need until you have the confidence to proceed. Then let your soaring spirit take you the rest of the way. Spirit wants to be your partner here. What brings joy to your soul is God; what does not is not.

Let your life count for something now, not in 2025. Push past the boundaries of self-awareness, spiritual growth and family relations to make an impact. Yes, these are all good things to focus on—but you can do much, much more. God is waiting for you to step up to the plate. The power you have to influence the world is limitless. Do not doubt that for a minute.

When you get outside self to serve others and the world at large, you are using the glory of Spirit to shift consciousness. Change at least one area of planet Earth with your unique, wonderful, powerful love. You will be assisted by a multitude of angels every time you offer yourself in service to others.

What gets you in the gut? Starving children? Hate towards one group or another? Animal abuse? There are certain issues in this world that are so dark, and need love and resolution so badly, that it's easy to get immobilized with pain. I have found myself so caught up and defeated by pain it seems easier to crawl in a corner and sob. Needless to say, this does not get anybody anywhere. What the pain can provide is the impetus to do something that lifts dark into light.

Does anything arouse similar feelings of anguish in your soul? Think carefully. That's where you can make the most difference. Casting out your strong reaction to one issue or another, taking a stand on it in private only, or weeping about the pain of it all is not what the universe needs from you.

One human being who used his outrage to effect change is a young man from Toronto, Ontario, Canada. After reading about child labor abuses, he used his pain to attempt to eradicate child slavery. He was only 12-years-old.

This now teenager has traveled the world—met with prime ministers, the Queen of England and even the Pope—but his focus remains singular: Change the world by helping the children.

When asked what it felt like to meet each of these important people, the young man remained polite but focused. Noting that while it was an honor, he was really more concerned about what each of them would do to "help the cause."

It's erroneous to think you must be on the world stage or have a public persona to make a difference. While a few of our fellow souls do travel the high profile road, that's where their higher self and the universe need them to be. You, too, may be on the world stage. Or you may work quietly in your community. If it is your intent to serve, you will be moved into a position where it is for the highest good of you and those you will be assisting.

In the meantime, know that anything you touch with love has the same power to transform lives as does the celebrity, politician or businessperson who commits to touch lives with love.

Take the most mundane of activities. The most inconsequential of acts—driving down the street or cleaning your house—has the power to light the world. Even cooking can impart love. Think of the movie "Like Water for Chocolate." Infuse your soul into food. Most of us don't have that intent, especially when we're just trying to get a meal on the table. But the next time you *want* to cook for someone, consciously put your energy into it. Imagine the person for whom you're cooking smiling and laughing, and feeling the love in their food.

If you want to infuse anything with the highest organizing principle of the universe—love—start by coming from a place of serenity. Struggling through a recipe or doing anything because it's a should do offsets your good intentions. Wait until there is joy in the moment. Then ask Spirit to work through you. Commit to transmit joy through your hands. Relax and breathe deeply. Put on music you like. Enjoy the process.

Do you doubt your hands have the power to transmit love? Think about how you touch a baby. Now think about how you touch your steering wheel after someone cuts you off. Which pair of hands would you rather have cooking for you?

If and when you proceed to serve others,
regardless of your own circumstances, your
problems will be put in their proper perspective.

One of the most touching stories of inanimate object love infusion is the tale of Athena Demetrios and her blankets. This grandmother's slogan is "blanket the world with love." Her Los Angeles-based company grew from Demetrios' belief that objects can and do transmit love. So she personally blesses each blanket. Then Demetrios and her staff attach an individual note of heartfelt love and donate the blankets to suffering children around the world. Some blankets are also sold through select retail outlets. Salespeople claim they fly off the shelves.

According to a report in the *Los Angeles Times*, doctors have seen miraculous results when children are wrapped in Demetrios' blankets.

So which blanket would you want your child to be wrapped in? A blanket from a chain store? Or a blanket blessed with love? I think we all know the answer. Even the most cynical among us understands the power of love.

The power that is in Athena Demetrios is the same power within you. You do not need a worldwide platform to transform lives in a big way. Imagine this scenario played out in your community—to wrap preemies at your local hospital, for example. You and your friends could knit or buy blankets, then collectively visualize the souls whose lives would be transformed by your efforts. Touch and affirm that each blanket wraps another child with the healing power of love. Create a ceremony of light.

None of us has the power to exist without affecting others. Whether we do so with love, indifference or malice is entirely up to us. Sometimes our own problems seem so insurmountable they divert our attention from what really matters. If and when you proceed to serve others, regardless of your own circumstances, your problems will be put in their proper perspective.

It is true that you must fill up with what you need spiritually. Serve from a full plate—meaning that self-love is paramount. Self-love, however, is not the same as self-involved. Self-love comes from a place of deep security and connection with Spirit. Self-involved comes from a position of perceived lack: lack of trust, lack of love, and lack of ability to remember what's real and what's illusion.

If you think you're straddling the boundary between self-love and self-involved, use this as a litmus test. Do you validate other people's feelings? Can you really listen with your heart? Shutting yourself off from hearing the other person's truth because it is not your reality is not behavior born of love.

Do you always have to be right? What's right for you may not be what's right for someone else. We are each children of God. You may have made different decisions from the homeless man or woman on the street, but in God's eyes we are all the same. Choices are neither right nor wrong. Some paths are more perilous, it's true, because they are constructed from fear. Other choices are easier because they are birthed from love. All paths lead back to God, though, and the choice each soul makes about how to get there is perfect for them.

Do not think yourself above others because society may have elevated you based on your charm, intellect, looks— or whatever other gifts have been chosen by you and our Creator. Nor are you less than anyone else either. You are beautiful. You are exquisite. Cherish what you have, rejoice in all your mental and physical assets. Then remind yourself how special your neighbor is and the murderer in prison. We are all one.

It's easy to turn away from things we do not feel comfortable confronting. Most of us find it easier to judge than to help. How many times do we avoid the eyes of panhandler? "Oh, he'll just buy more booze" or "She's on crack, I'm not going to help perpetuate *that* cycle." That person is you and that person is me, separated by a very thin line of choices. Do not turn away or close your heart. Give what you can without thought for what will happen next. After you give, it is no longer your concern. This is exactly where this person needs to be right now. None of us is going to save anyone by refusing to put a dollar in their pocket.

If you have little to give in terms of money, share a sandwich. Or simply send love. Mentally say, "I send you light. You are loved." or whatever feels comfortable. Their soul will hear you. And they will absolutely be elevated by the encounter.

You are exquisite. Cherish what you have;
rejoice in your mental and physical assets. Then
remind yourself how special your neighbor is and the
murderer in prison. We are all one.

When someone speaks to you from their heart—whether it's a street person, family member or coworker—and you turn away without listening you are responding from fear. Your soul is asking you to see things differently. If you turn away, you've lost an opportunity to connect with someone who needs you.

Perhaps you are afraid that at some level you will have to accept responsibility once you acknowledge someone else's pain. This is true both in general terms—that is, the plight of the disadvantaged in society, as well as it pertains to more intimate relations.

The reality: You are free as soon as you connect with love instead of defensiveness. "The truth will set you free" is not a meaningless axiom. When you are ready to own whatever pain you've caused, directly or indirectly, the first person who gets healed is yourself. On the other hand, you will stay self-involved as long as you discount truth, your own and others.

Owning is not the same as being guilty. Taking responsibility is not the same as self-flagellation. Blame and guilt are not the issues here. Healing is. A commitment to heal the past by walking through it again—quietly and with introspection—is all that's needed.

"A life unexamined is a life not worth living." Remember this proverb. Without reflection your growth is impeded. Return to Spirit is exhausting. And real joy, versus joy from external pursuits, is always just beyond grasp.

When a group in society has been wronged, it is very much like when a child in a family has been hurt. No one wants to take responsibility. The mantra becomes, "What's over is over." Lack of validation perpetuates the problem.

With that denial comes acting out, or bad behavior, from the aggrieved group or child.

In the United States, for example, white people are loathe to harken back to the days of slavery. The general view is, what's the point? It wasn't me, it was my ancestors...what's done is done...let's get together and live in peace. These seem like valid sentiments, superficially. This is not, however, how people learn to love each other again.

For healing to be real there has to be a meeting of the minds, an understanding of the other person's pain. Sometimes the only thing that will get the job done is a heartfelt apology. Not a lip service apology. An apology that comes from the heart—with a corresponding regret for what has transpired—is what heals.

Every student who studies pre-Civil War history should be shackled and bid for in a mock slave auction. Sound horrendous? Yes...*but it was horrendous*. Show young people what slavery felt like. Few adults have felt it because most people in the white community do not want to revisit the horror of what our ancestors brought to bear. So let's start with the children.

One teacher in New York state actually tried something similar and was fired. That's too bad. Because when you are in someone else's shoes, even for an hour, your life can be forever altered.

And why should we as a society even consider an exercise like this? Because even in this new millennium, Black candidates with equal experience and education are routinely passed over for jobs, denied housing opportunities and even treated differently at the dry cleaner's. Still many Caucasians deny. Why? Because no one wants to own the responsibility that comes from validating the pain.

A Fortune 500 company with top executives openly spewing racial hatred—taped for the whole world to hear—makes big news. Then the story dies away. Once again, the mantra begins: "African Americans have equal opportunity and there is no discrimination. Anything that would indicate otherwise is an anomaly."

Tolerance for people who are different from ourselves has been around a long time. Some practice it, some do not. Tolerance is a lot different than love. Tolerance is "all people should be treated equally." Then your daughter comes home with a man of a different race. Are you filled with love? Tolerance is "what people do in the privacy of their bedroom is their own business." Then your son announces he's gay. Do you embrace his life with love?

Tolerance is a beginning, but it is not *the* answer to where we as a human race need to be. Love is. It is the strongest force of the universe. It is the only force that binds us, casts out the darkness and propels us forward as a group of light beings. And that's what we are: One Group. If you think you are separated from someone else on the basis of skin color, socioeconomic status or any other superficial quality, that is part of the illusion you've created. And that illusion is carrying you further and further away from Source.

When you are not listening to and loving others, you're only giving to yourself. And self-involved is a lonely place to be because no one wants to be there with you.

Love knows no artificial boundaries constructed on the basis of skin color or any other so-called difference. We are all one. If you can't "get that" and you don't want to suffer in order to remember it, listen with your heart. Find a reference point in your own life when you were judged, condemned or lived in fear. Then respond to people who continue to be devalued on the basis of something irrelevant, accordingly.

We can't all transform ourselves into a person with a different skin color, like the author of *Black Like Me*. Nor can we adopt a different sexual orientation or live as the other gender. (Although some have tried the latter.) By looking for parallel experiences in our own past, however, we can connect with similar feelings of fear or persecution.

One older white man could not relate to the Black experience. So he was encouraged to remember the fear and humiliation he felt when his father used to beat him. This man had no idea what it felt like to be treated like a second class citizen in the United States.

When asked to recall what went on with his father, the experience returned to him with the corresponding feelings of inner rage. He conjured the sickening feeling not only of being beaten but of having the abuse denied. Eureka. By accessing his own pain, this man was able to connect—if only for a heartbeat—with what it feels like to be an African American in this society.

Groups that are in the minority, without a power base, are at a disadvantage. No surprise there. Even Canada—a model for tolerance and multiculturalism—has yet to solve its deeply-rooted French versus English problem. Quebec, with "Je me souviens" on its license plates, sums up the collective energy in that province. The translated "I remember" is a not-so-subtle reminder to English Canadians that French Canadians will not forget the attempts to quash francophone language and culture.

English Canadians, many of whom are weary of trying to reconcile, say the exact opposite is what has occurred.

While some francophones remain committed to federalism, a significant number of others want sovereignty. And still other French Canadians believe the 1960's book *White Niggers of North America* continues to apply. So the mutual resentment continues.

The desire to be heard is universal. What goes on at the national or international level mirrors the same polarization that occurs between families and friends. Once pain is validated, instead of being discounted or minimized, we heal what divides us—whether as a country or as a family. No one's feelings are wrong; feelings simply are. No matter how uncomfortable you or your neighbor may be looking them squarely in the face, they are real. And they need to be faced for healing to occur.

The universe will continue to push each of us into a space where we view everyone as equals. It will start in our own backyard.

Is it the alcoholic street person near your place of business who bothers you? Perhaps it's the homosexual teacher who coaches your daughter, the interracial couple who moved in next door, your dentist with AIDS or your crazy relative. If any of these people scare you, look again. We are One.

How can you love everybody? How can you not love everybody if we all come from the same Source? It's like the expression, "Well, I don't really love my arm because it's different from my leg." It's all you. And together we make up the composite whole, which is God.

You don't have to run out and save the world. You do, however, have to save yourself from bigotry and judgment and intolerance. If you do not, you close your heart. And you cast the light that is you in a shroud of darkness.

God gives us free will. If we choose to remember our way back to what is real by dabbling in what is not real—fear, hate and indifference—that's our prerogative. Spirit will not take away your chosen experience. If you think you must create such estrangement from yourself and Spirit in order to fully appreciate that you are in fact, light and love and all that is glorious, that's okay.

The problem is joy and peace do not coexist with hate and fear. Turmoil is one way to get back to the Divine but it's a long and laborious trip. And you may find yourself surrounded by some strange bedfellows along the way. If you are tired of the struggle, remember who you are by living in love every day of your life.

You are perfect. Joy and love are your birthright. If you have been taken away from this knowledge and do not believe it to be so, reconnect with what is Truth today. Snuggle in God's arms. "I forgot who I am. Now I remember. I am All That Is."

> *How can you not love everybody if we all*
> *come from the same Source? It's like the expression,*
> *"Well, I really don't love my arm because*
> *it's different from my leg."*

Listen to yourself and others with compassion. Gently turn over those painful areas of your life to the light. It's that simple. No prayer is unheard, no request for transformation denied.

If, however, you continue to come from a place that has not yet been lit by love, the universe will make it increasingly uncomfortable for you. God is trying to show you a better way to live. Your soul is attempting to redirect you to an easier path. Closed heart equals self-involved. When you're not listening to and loving others, you are only giving to yourself. And self-involved is a lonely place to be because no one wants to be there with you.

Open to receive the gifts only others can bring. These may include the gift of self-awareness, an understanding of other people's pain or simply the gift of love. Let these gifts heal you—and free you—from being stuck at a deep level of self-condemnation and isolation from Spirit.

There's a camp in the mountains of Southern California that works with kids in high school to remind them of the fundamental maxim: "Treat others as you want to be treated." These camps are conducted all over the country under the auspices of the National Conference for Community and Justice (NCCJ). One part of the program: Alleviate gender tensions by allowing kids to "feel" how the other half lives.

In one scenario girls line up on either side of a hallway. Male students walk by to cat-calls, salacious comments and groping. (Similar to what many girls endure every day of the school year.) The pain and humiliation these young men feel is shockingly real. Some of the boys break down and cry. What is going to change unwanted behavior? This kind of exercise? Or an intellectual discussion of sexual harassment?

Not unlike the idea of shackling students so they "feel" the bondage of slavery and the dehumanization of human auctions, it works. Teenagers do not always have the emotional resources to empathize. Role playing to see how it feels to be harassed because you're a woman, a geek,

Hispanic, Jewish…or whatever is being persecuted at that particular school…makes the point powerfully.

Parents hold the highest hopes for their children, not just to be successful, but to be kind and compassionate people. There is one other element, however, that often gets forgotten in the teaching of children—and that is courage.

Teach your children to go out on a limb on behalf of someone who is being unjustly treated. Regardless of what repercussions come their way, your children need to know that stepping out from the crowd to help another person is always right.

Love is immediately introduced into any situation when just one person has the courage to intervene. *Teach your child to be that one person.* Whether it is defending someone spoken about in a derogatory manner—or literally extending a hand to a persecuted party—it needs to be done.

When the element of fear comes into play, and at the core of all persecutory behavior there is fear, people huddle together like sheep afraid to move away from the crowd and incur the wrath of the persecutor. Teach your children that it's okay to stand alone against the darkness—away from behavior that is not light. Historically we all know that lives can be saved when there are those among us willing to operate from love, no matter what the cost.

In our day-to-day living we may not be called upon to be heroes. We do, however, need to react with kindness and compassion as we move through the day. One postal official I regularly encountered was a surly old guy who snapped and growled. I had read about something similar: A woman, frustrated by her pharmacist's rude attitude, discovered his wife was dying of cancer. My postal worker's behavior was extremely off-putting...who knew his story? Maybe his wife had an incurable disease, too. I tried my best to smile and not let his rudeness affect my day.

A few months later his name came up in conversation with another postal representative. "He must have a rough personal life," I ventured. "No. He just doesn't believe in customer service," was the response. "Oh, I thought maybe his wife had cancer or something." "His wife is fine!" the other postal worker responded with hoots of laughter. Oh well, who knew? That's the point. You just don't know.

Err on the side of kindness and give everyone the benefit of the doubt. Even with this case in point, who knows what childhood pain the guy was carrying with him? You don't need to be psychoanalyzing people on the street, but it's never wrong to respond with love where you see shades of darkness.

Love. It is the only force that binds us,
casts out the darkness and propels us forward
as a group of light beings.

Remember this rule of thumb: In your day-to-day existence give on the little things, hold fast on the big ones. Let your spouse pick the television program or restaurant. Fill up the gas tank, replace the toilet paper, walk the dog, offer to baby-sit for a neighbor, tell someone you love them, be considerate...Listen to other people with your heart. Hear their story. If they are open to receive, give them your soul light.

If they are not, send them love and let them do with it as they wish.

How you live your life, whom you choose for your partner, the career path you pursue, what you do with your
body, the values you espouse…these are choices that can
only be made by you. Sometimes it may conflict with
what others hold dear. And that's okay. The *only* voice that
is important is your inner voice. Because that is the voice
of God calling you Home.